MW00654672

How to Wolf-Proof Your Kids

A Practical Guide for Keeping Your Kids Catholic

GARY G. MICHUTA

Except where otherwise indicated, all Scripture quotations in this book are taken from the *New American Bible with Revised New Testament and Revised Psalms* © 1991, 1986, 1970 Confraternity of Christian Doctrine, Washington, DC, and are used by permission of the copyright owner. All Rights Reserved. No part of the *New American Bible* may be reproduced in any form without permission in writing from the copyright owner.

Cover art by Mimi Sternhagen
Cover design by Daniel Grejek

How to Wolf-proof Your Kids

© 2009 by Gary G. Michuta. All rights reserved.
Published by Nikaria Press
Livonia, Michigan
734-674-0676
www.HandsOnApologetics.com

Printed in the United States of America

Library of Congress Cataloguing-in-Publication Data

Michuta, Gary G., 1964 –
How To Wolf-proof Your Kids / Gary G. Michuta
Includes bibliographical references and indexes.
ISBN: 978-0-9988399-0-5

Contents

Acknowledgments

There are many people that I would like to acknowledge for their help and encouragement that helped make *How to Wolf-proof Your Kids* possible. I extend my deepest gratitude to Robert Salmon for his encouragement and support for this project. Robert is an unsung hero in the apologetics world and he deserves to be recogonized for his unbound charity and wisdom. A debt of thanks is owed to the good people at The Grotto Press for bringing this book to market, especially Paul and Cassandra Husak. I would like to thank the many friends and colleagues whose advice, insights, and example helped me be a better apologist for Christ and his Church and bring about the genesis of this book, especially Patrick Madrid, Robert Corzine, Dan Eagen, William Albrecht, Stephen Ray, David Armstrong, Timothy Staples, John Martigoni, and Thomas McGlynn. I also give my warm thanks to Daniel Grejek and Mimi Sternhagen for their generosity and wonderful artistic contributions. Finally, I would like to thank my family, Christine, Paulina, Daniel, and Jennifer for their many sacrifices.

Introduction

"Hello. I was wondering if you could help me. Our daughter just told us that she is leaving the Church."

As a Catholic apologist, I am a person who explains, defends, and helps people understand the Catholic Faith. It is an eye-opening experience because I am called in whenever or wherever someone's faith is being attacked. Catholic apologetics can be incredibly rewarding. It also has its heartbreaks. The worst of these heartbreaks begins with a phone call or an e-mail, like the one above, from a parent whose child has been pulled out of the Church.

Notice that I said *pulled out* of the Church, not *left* the Church. When people become disenchanted with the Faith or lose interest in practicing the religion of their upbringing, they leave. Others leave not because they originally want to do so, but because anti-Catholic missionaries recruit them into their own group. These Catholics were the victims of sheep-stealing.

Sheep-stealing occurs when someone uses illegitimate or manipulative means to pull another person out of their current Faith and into the recruiter's own church, group, sect, or cult. Before anyone attempted to pull Catholics out of the Church, that perhaps had no intention whatsoever of ever leaving their Faith; in fact, they were quite happy where they were. Through social manipulation, half-truths, distortions, and suppressed information critical of the recruiter's group, these Catholics' views of the Church were poisoned. The sheep-stealers used these elements to pressure their victims to leave the Church and commit to their group.

As an apologist, I'm not as concerned about people who *left* the Church. To be sure, such cases are tragic in that these Catholics are throwing away something priceless, and I urge them to reconsider their decision. Such actions, however, can't be prevented except to ensure that these Catholics know what they are giving up.

What concerns me more is sheep-stealing. These Catholics were pulled out of the Church on false pretenses, deceived into leaving. Quite frankly, the deception wasn't very difficult to achieve. Deficiencies in education and religious formation make it quite easy for anti-Catholic recruiters to distort and twist truths to make vulnerable Catholics leave the Church. Yet Catholics don't have to be defenseless. Sheep-stealing can be prevented if potential victims have the proper set of skills and knowledge to make recruiting more difficult.

Understanding the deficiencies that contributed to successful sheep-stealing is quite easy. Over the years, I've spoken to literally hundreds of former Catholics who had become anti-Catholic. Regardless of whether these former Catholics became atheists, agnostics, Muslims, Protestants, or joined a pseudo-Christian cult or sect, nearly all share the same deficiencies in their Catholic upbringing and formation. Recruiters exploited these deficiencies and when these former Catholics, in turn, tried to pull others out of the Church. Guess what they exploit? You guessed it. They use the same tactics that were used against them. There is not only a commonality among the victims of sheep-stealers, but also a commonality among the sheep-stealers themselves. We will call them wolves.

It makes sense doesn't it? Wolves stick to what works. Anti-Catholic wolves, although differing from one another in beliefs and ideology, use essentially the same method of recruitment.

Armed with knowledge, however, Catholic parents and educators can take preventative steps, especially when their children are young and developing, to correct deficiencies and make the recruiting process much more difficult for anti-Catholic wolves. In other words, Catholic parents must "wolf-proof" their children.

Even if you follow all this book's suggestions, does "wolf-proofing" mean your children will never fall victim to sheep-stealing? No, it does not. Instead, wolf-proofing should be understood as giving your child all the necessary skills and know-how to make the chance of being deceived and thus recruitment less likely.

About this Book

This book is the product of years of work in the field of apologetics and evangelism. A few years ago, I gathered my experiences and ideas into a series of talks titled "How to Wolf-proof Your Kids." Catholic parents around the country were extremely enthusiastic about the talks. Parents frequently approached me after my talks and encouraged me to put the information into book form because their own experiences so closely mirrored what I said. Some of these parents would proceed to share their own heart-breaking stories when their child had been pulled out of the Church. These discussions with parents also helped me to decide what information to include in my talks. I took these parents' advice to heart and the result is this book.

Here's how: I have worked to make this book as short as possible. There are no footnotes and few technical terms. Although *How to Wolf-proof Your Kids* is short, it is packed with information and insights that I think will be helpful for parents.

The book covers five important topics.

Chapter 1 – Who Should Be Afraid of the Big Bad Wolf?

The book begins by introducing the reader to the wolves. When I was growing up, I didn't know there were such things as anti-Catholic ministries and sheep-stealing. I suspect some Catholic parents are unaware of these wolves as well. This chapter will help you, the parent, know what you are battling.

Chapter 2 – Going on the Hunt: Seven Easy Steps to Sheep-stealing

Sheep-stealing is a process. Like most processes, recruiting is comprised of different stages. Each stage is designed to manipulate and inculcate the beliefs of the recruiter's group and pressure the recruit to shift his or her commitment. We will explore seven typical stages that comprise the process of recruitment and how each stage affects the victim's perceptions.

Chapter 3 – Wolf-proofing Your Kids

Building upon what we've learned about recruiting, this chapter will give you concrete suggestions to empower your children to recognize and resist being pulled out of the Church.

Chapter 4 – What to Do If Your Child is Being Recruited

The recruiting process can be very stealthy, even well-prepared children can slip into the process without knowing it. This chapter contains advice that will give you a distinct advantage in rescuing their children from whoever is recruiting them. You will learn how to spot the early signs of recruitment, what to do, and what not to do when rescuing your child.

Chapter 5 – What to Do If Your Child has Already Left

Losing a child to an anti-Catholic recruiter can be one of the most heart-breaking and devastating events Catholic parents suffer. Chapter 5 will look at what you can do to bring back children who have already left the Church. The Chapter will also contain a short discussion on Apologetic Postures that will apply to all parents who need to rescue their children.

You'll find *How to Wolf-proof Your Kids* packed with practical advice and suggestions drawn from my own experience and others in the field. Remember, however, that this book includes only suggestions. It is up to you, the Catholic parent, to decide what will work best for you and how to adapt and apply these suggestions to fit your family's needs.

As a further help, several appendices provide you with additional recommendations, referrals, and resources that you may need to help wolf-proof your kids. These recommendations will save you time, money, and frustration.

It is my hope that this book will supply all Catholic parents and educators with thought-provoking suggestions, strategies, and skills that they need to empower their children to stand up to less-than-honorable proselytizers and be a witness to God's truth and love.

Chapter 1 – Who Should Be Afraid of the Big Bad Wolf?

Joe and Betty Tutti grew up Catholic. Both came from devoted Italian and Polish families who loved the Faith and did their best to live it. When Joe and Betty had their first child, Julie, they wanted to give her the same warm, solid Catholic upbringing they had received from their parents. They scrimped and saved to send her to Catholic schools. They never missed Mass on Sundays and Holy Days. Overall they lived a joyous Catholic life. They did everything right - or so they thought.

One day Julie returned from college a different person. She announced she would no longer be attending Mass because she had become convinced that Catholicism was a false religion leading people to Hell. Joe and Betty were dumbfounded. "This can't be our daughter," they thought and looked at each other confused and dismayed. Julie had changed. She was no longer the sweet, fun-loving, care-free girl Joe and Betty once knew and loved. The "new" Julie had become somber, humorless, judgmental, and hostile to practically everything she once held sacred.

"Maybe she is just going through some sort of phase," Joe and Betty concluded. They assumed their daughter would "grow out of it" and everything would go back to normal. At first, their strategy seemed to work. Peace had more or less been restored to the Tutti household until Julie got married and had children. Suddenly, things began to change for the worse.

Julie and her husband made it clear they did *not* intend to raise their kids Catholic. Moreover, they were cool to the idea of letting Joe and Betty, a pair of Catholics, visit their children. At first, however, Julie allowed Joe and Betty to see the babies whenever they wanted. When the children began to grow, visitations became more and more restricted. Eventually, the only time Joe and Betty were allowed to see their grandchildren was at their daughter's church-sponsored events. Many of these functions required the Tuttis to sit through long, boring sermons and lectures laced with anti-Catholic diatribes.

On one occasion – a rare moment – Julie allowed Betty to see her grandchildren unaccompanied. During the visit, Betty learned what Julie and her husband had been telling the children. The children had been led to believe that Joe and Betty were deceived by Satan and were going to Hell unless they switched religions. Betty lost her cool. She confronted Julie and a big argument ensued. The argument ended with Julie and her husband telling Betty that she and Joe were no longer welcome to see their grandkids, ever!

The drive home from Julie's house was sad and sobering. Joe and Betty felt sick. They felt as if their daughter, the real Julie, had somehow died. She died along with their dreams of sharing the rest of their lives together with their grandchildren in a loving family. Over and over, they asked themselves, "How could our daughter have turned against us like this?"

The answer to Joe and Betty's question is, sadly simple. Their daughter didn't turn against them; she was stolen from them. Julie didn't go away to college with the notion that she would reject everything she held sacred as a Catholic. Julie was recruited, indoctrinated, and pressured into committing to an anti-Catholic group. Through social manipulation, half-truths, and outright deceptions, her views on Catholicism were poisoned and replaced with different beliefs. In short, Julie was a sheep stolen by wolves.

Sheep? Wolves? What's this talk about livestock? The imagery is drawn from Scripture. Jesus called the members of His Church His "sheep" and His "flock" (Matthew 9:36, 18:12-13, 26:31, *et al.*). Christ is the Good Shepherd (John 10:11, 14) and He appointed the apostles to be shepherds (or pastors) over His flock (John 21:16-17). Moreover, Jesus warned his followers to beware of wolves who dress themselves up in sheep's clothing. These wolves are called "false prophets" (Matthew 7:15) or false teachers who will attack the flock. Indeed, some wolves even rise up from within the flock to "draw disciples away after them" (Acts. 20:28-30). The idea of wolves and sheep-stealing is nothing new or novel. Our Lord warned us about these things.

Speaking of wolves, it is important to define what we mean. In this book, a wolf is a person, usually an anti-Catholic, who uses illegitimate and deceptive means to manipulate unsuspecting Catholics to leave the Faith of their upbringing and join their own particular church, denomination, group, sect, or cult. Deception is their main mode of operation; therefore, the biblical idea of "wolves in sheep's clothing" fits the subject of this book nicely.

Sheep-stealing and Its Effects

Back in the early 1990s, when I began my odyssey in Catholic apologetics, I was shocked to find dozens of national, full-time, anti-Catholic ministries dedicated to pulling Catholics out of the Church. Don't think that anti-Catholic wolves are restricted to the local fundamentalist church down the road; they constitute a large variety of beliefs from pseudo-Christian groups (*e.g.*, Jehovah's Witnesses, the Church of Jesus Christ of Latter-day Saints [Mormons]), the New Age Movement, and others) and non-Christian religions (*e.g.*, Islam, paganism, Wicca, and others). We can also add to this list the ever-present toxic media, secular humanism, and atheism. Unfortunately, the list can go on and on.

Despite their numbers, wolves rarely make a blip on the parental early warning radar. Parents usually have bigger and more immediate worries such as which high school their child will attend or to what college or university they will be accepted. To be sure, these are important issues. A good education is important in preparing children for life in the business world.

Think beyond business for a moment, however. Who among us would expect a child to succeed in the "real world" with only an eighth-grade education? I venture to say that no one with a straight face could honestly expect a child to succeed with such a paltry education. Yet millions of Catholic parents send their children into the "real world" with only an eighth-grade appreciation of their Faith! Even worse, they do this with the expectation that their children will succeed in living out an authentic Catholic life. Is it any wonder that thousands of Catholics are pulled out of the Church each year? Indeed, perhaps it is a wonder. The number should really be much higher.

Why does this disconnect exist between secular education and religious education? I don't know. A business man or woman with only an eighth-grade appreciation of business will surely be incapable of functioning. Does it not make sense that a man or a woman with only an eighth-grade appreciation of their Faith will not be very capable either? Perhaps the problem lies in the fact that Catholic parents are more aware of wolves in the market place than wolves with designs on religion, philosophy, or ideology. Parents might also assume that because their own religious education stopped at a young age and they remained faithful, their children will do the same.

Joe and Betty seemed to have held on to this idea. What parents don't realize is that the world has changed drastically since their childhood. Wolves are much more pernicious because the world has grown smaller. Today, one person can influence literally hundreds of people through a popular Web page or blog. Moreover, wolves have improved their recruitment techniques over the years. Just a few decades ago, wolves were easily identified and relatively easy to avoid. Today, however, they have become stealthier and more sophisticated in how they recruit people out of the Church. What worked for you may very well *not* work for your children.

What has remained the same are the destructive effects of losing a child through sheep-stealing. As we read in the opening story, families suffer almost as much as the victims. It is not unusual to see children turn against their own family. Peace is destroyed; dreams are shattered. Family gatherings become war zones. Even when the child returns to the Church, the years lost with your child and your grandchildren are gone forever. Sheep-stealing affects everyone.

Over the years, I have received hundreds of phone calls and e-mails from concerned parents who lost their child to anti-Catholic predators. More often than not, these parents were not aware that their child was being recruited - much less that they were thinking of leaving the Faith - until their child announced his or her intention to do so. By that time, their child had already undergone a lengthy process that involved indoctrination and inculcation of the wolves' worldview. Their child was ready to commit to the group.

When the cat is out of the bag and parents finally find out their child no longer wants to be Catholic, the parents' first reactions are typically counter-productive. They may, in fact, inadvertently re-affirm their child's new belief system. Instead of "talking sense into their child," these parental missteps drive their child deeper and deeper into their new belief system until meaningful conversation on religion becomes almost impossible. It is often at this point that parents seek a competent apologist. By this point, so much damage has been done that subsequent interventions are often doomed to failure.

Doing the right thing at the right time can dramatically increase your success in rescuing a loved one. But is there anything that parents can do *before* this happens? In other words, is it possible for parents to wolf-proof their kids?

Can Children Really Be Wolf-proof?

The answer depends on your definition of wolf-proofing. If you mean making it impossible for a child to be recruited out of the Church, I'm afraid the answer is no. Faith is a gift from God (Ephesians 2:8) and like all gifts one can throw it away. If, however, you mean the actions a parent takes to equip his child with skills and knowledge that make it very difficult for an anti-Catholic to pull that child out of the Church, the answer is yes, absolutely.

First, consider that there are many different kinds of wolves out there. Wolves can be Christians, non-Christians, pseudo-Christians, atheists, secularists, pagans and witches. The prospect of developing a single set of preventive measures, therefore, is daunting. Moreover, even within the categories above, there is a remarkable diversity from group to group. For example, some wolves prefer to hunt in packs (such as churches, groups, and fellowships). Others prefer to hunt as an unaffiliated lone wolf. Some wolves have favorite hunting grounds, such as university campuses, lecture halls, doughnut shops, alcohol and drug rehab centers, and self-help groups. Others recruit indirectly through films, television, books, and other media. Wolves also differ from one another in their approach to recruiting. Some wolves go door-to-door; others use "non-denominational" Bible studies; still others use Web sites, blogs, and other online media. Given such a wide variety of aggressors, how can a parent wolf-proof his child from all of these diverse groups?

One salient fact makes wolf-proofing actually possible. Wolves, like everyone else, will stick to what works best. Although *what* a wolf may try to indoctrinate may differ quite a bit from wolf to wolf, *how* wolves recruit their victims is remarkably similar. Even among the most coercive cults, which employ thought-reform or mind-control techniques, the *process of recruiting* has similarities to those used by other less coercive groups. Parents who want to learn how to wolf-proof their kids, therefore, must first learn, at least in outline form, what is typically involved in the recruiting. Once you've learned how recruitment works, you can formulate strategies to counteract the recruitment process.

Summary

To protect your child adequately from anti-Catholic wolves or recruiters, you must understand the essentials:

- Learn how the recruiting process generally works.
- Know how you can intervene in the recruiting process and rescue your children. Recognize the tell-tale signs that your child is being recruited.
- Drawing from what you learn from the points above, formulate a strategy to enhance your child's education and religious formation to make him less likely to become a victim of anti-Catholic predators.

In the following chapters, we will address each of these steps in detail. Scenarios illustrate what happens when the correct steps are taken and what happens when they are not. These senerios are constructed from actual events and each is followed by a short analysis to highlight important observations and principles of which you should be aware. Each chapter also contains helpful hints and concrete suggestions on how to best implement the information and skills in your home.

This book's appendices contain information on recommended reading and ministries. These appendices provide valuable advice that will save you time, money, and effort in putting together a good wolf-proofing curriculum and preparing for a successful intervention.

Effective Wolf-proofing

All the hints and suggestions in this book will be useless unless you put them into practice. You know your child's abilities and aptitudes better than anyone in the world does. It is up to you to take this information and modify it to make it appropriate for your child's age and ability. This book's suggestions are not one-size-fits-all applications. They need to be tailored to each individual child to ensure that skills develop naturally and his knowledge base grows in a way that makes sense to him. For Catholic parents whose children go to public or private schools, these suggestions will need to be added to enhance their current education and religious formation. Homeschooling parents may need to decide which suggestions fit best within their home curriculum and which suggestions would work best outside of school time. For professional Catholic educators, this book may be helpful for enhancing your students' Catholic curriculum. With imagination, you can turn these tips and suggestions into a natural, fun, everyday routine that you and your family will enjoy.

Something to Remember while Reading this Book

Children and parents should not be afraid of the big, bad wolves of anti-Catholicism. They should be aware, however, that wolves are out there. As such, parents should prepare their children, the best they can, to fend off these wolves when the occasion presents itself. We should be as Our Lord advised His disciples to be when he sent them out as sheep in the midst of wolves; "Be shrewd as serpents and simple as doves" (Matthew 10:16).

Chapter 2 –Going on the Hunt: Seven Easy Steps to Sheep-stealing

"It takes a thief to catch a thief." If one knows how he will be robbed, he could take steps to prevent the theft. Likewise, the best way to prevent a wolf from pulling your child, friend, or relative out of the Church is to know how wolves' steal sheep. Once the recruiting process is understood, you can make each step of the process more difficult for wolves. In other words, the first step of wolf-proofing is to learn how wolves hunt.

Step #1 - Target a Sheep

Sheep-stealing is a process, not a single chance encounter. The first step in sheep-stealing is to identify a potential recruit. Catholics in particular are often singled out for several reasons.

Truth Claims

Because the Catholic Church is the one true Church established by Jesus Christ to teach, sanctify, and govern in His name, Catholics are orientated to believe in objective truth and that truth can be accessed through the historic Church. If the legitimate authority can be done away with, then *all* other systems (including those who make no pretense of having any historic connection to Christ) are a possible replacement.

Sacramental Hunger

Catholics, through Baptism and the other Sacraments, are given a deep inclination towards God; we know God and we wish to know Him more; we love God and we wish to grow deeper in His love; we are in union with God and we wish to grow in an ever deeper union with Him. Even nominal Catholics are given, through the Sacraments, a special capacity for faith, hope, and love. Therefore, even when non-practicing Catholics desire to know and love God. Indeed, the desire likely will intensify during times of neglect just as a well-fed person's hunger may intensify when there is a reduction in food. Catholics (especially those who have fallen away from, rejected, or are ignorant of the Faith) may see the wolves as an attractive means of satisfying this deep religious inclination.

Presumption of Charity

Catholics do not view other religions (with the possible exception of Satanism) as enemies. Since Catholicism possesses the fullness of truth and grace, we charitably recognize that there are many elements of grace and truth that are shared in other religions. Catholics value these shared aspects, not only because they come from God, but because they provide us with a common platform for dialogue and possible reunion. However, only later Catholic education, in college or seminary, address the differences of other religions and belief systems. So many Catholics, who never read that level of religious education, have an irenic view of other faiths; they do not really understand how these faiths differ from one another and from Catholicism. Non-Catholic faiths and belief systems are therefore regarded as harmless. Wolves exploit this naiveté by gaining an uncritical hearing.

Religious Immaturity

It is a sad fact that many Catholics end their religious education after their eighth-grade Confirmation. Once this Sacrament is received they go into the world with the misconception that they have learned everything about their Faith. When challenged as an adult about what they believe, often Catholics either (1) refuse to discuss religion any further, (2) relegate religion to personal preference or feeling, or (3) consign what they learned in eight years of religious education to the pile of forlorn childhood fantasies like the tooth fairy and embrace what seems most intellectually satisfying. A well-trained wolf knows the first two responses well. The process of recruitment is designed to overcome both of them and move the recruit to the third category, rejecting their Faith and embracing the belief system that is being presented as a viable alternative.

Wolves use these traits to their own advantage. Stealth is the wolves' great weapon. Wolves don "sheep's clothing" for good reason. As you will see in the next section of this chapter, the recruiting process does not look at all like someone is trying to sheep-steal. Instead, the recruiting appears to be something considerably less alarming such as a kind stranger wishing to pass on biblical knowledge, share some enlightening tidbit, or plug a new friend into a social network. Wolves will make their actions appear to be everything but sheep-stealing. As far as the victim can see, the wolf appears completely harmless; they only want to be the victim's friend. Yes, they have become friends, but *for the purpose of recruitment.*

Hunting Season

One's vulnerability to exploitation changes throughout one's life. Wolves are aware of these periods of vulnerability and they tend to target recruits who are going through transitional stages in their lives. During these periods, one's support systems (close relationships with family and friends, the local church, friends at work, schoolmates, etc.) are usually strained and a clear cut vision of one's future is often blurred.

- Lost or started a job and/or changing one's occupation
- Lost a close friend or loved one, or been recently divorced
- Moved into a new home or unfamiliar area
- Begun attending a new school or university, especially one that is far from home
- Recently married or had children
- Been confined or restricted to the home

Such transitional phases offer wolves an opportunity to redirect the unsteady person to a path more favorable to the wolf's goals. People who are experiencing these challenges are more open to uncritically accepting whatever appears to offer a solution to their problems. For example, if you feel alone struggling with a difficulty, a well-groomed, religiously oriented, friendly stranger may seem to be a welcome opportunity for help and comfort. Because of your situation, the main question on your mind is *whether* this person will be my friend, not *why* this person is trying to be my friend. Thus, the wolf receives a pass into your social life.

Step #2 - Build a good relationship with a potential recruit

Once the wolf has found a target, the wolf befriends the potential victim. The second step may seem at first counter-intuitive. Shouldn't the next step be arguing why Catholicism is wrong? Some wolves do argue against Catholicism from the outset, but such an approach is rarely used because it rarely works. Even the most aggressive door-to-door missionaries do not start off with doctrine. True, they will knock at your door and ask a theologically loaded question, such as, "We've been taking a survey in your neighborhood to see if, in light of all the violence and wars, you believe God is still in control?" But the purpose of this question really is not to strike up a theological debate, but to see whether the person at the door is open to the missionaries' message. If the person is open to their message, a conversation ensues and an effort is made to start a "bible study." It is at the "bible study," not the doorstep that indoctrination begins.

Human beings are social animals, not robots. Wolves know that the most influential, non-cognitive, persuasive force that they can use is our need for social interaction and acceptance. Wanting to fit into a group is often more important to a person than whether a belief system is true. The following real-life scenario will illustrate the power of the subconscious desire to belong.

Scenario #1 – Going to College

The big day had finally arrived. Johnny had packed his bags and he was leaving home for college. Johnny had never been away from home before and being alone at college was new, exciting, and a little bit scary. A few of his friends from high school was going to the same school, but since the campus was so large and his friends were taking different classes, Johnny was pretty much on his own.

The first couple of weeks on campus were difficult; Johnny was surrounded by strangers. Eventually, a few faces began to look familiar. He recognized some of them from his classes and others from the cafeteria. One day, a classmate named Bill sat at Johnny's table in the cafeteria. Bill was a nicely dressed, clean-cut guy who always seemed to be surrounded by friends. The two struck up a conversation and talked about all sorts of things: where Johnny was from, what classes he was taking, which church he attended, and so on. Johnny and Bill soon became friends. Johnny wasn't like the rest of the kids in his dorm, he wasn't interested in "partying" and neither was Bill. In fact, Johnny often thought to himself, "I bet my mom and dad would love Bill, especially compared to all the partiers I could have befriended in the dorm."

Over the next few weeks, Bill introduced Johnny to his other friends. Johnny's new group of friends became his main source of entertainment and companionship. But there was a problem. Every Wednesday and Friday night, all of Johnny's new friends disappeared from campus to go to a Bible study. Johnny wasn't the least bit interested in studying the Bible, but his friends seemed to really enjoy it and they seemed very disappointed when Johnny refused their offer to come to the study. Eventually, Wednesdays and Fridays became pretty boring. Johnny thought, "A Bible-study can't be any more boring than sitting around my dorm all day. Maybe I should tag along with them. At least, I could still hang around my friends."

Johnny went to the next Bible study and it didn't seem as boring as he thought. Everyone was very nice and they seemed to enjoy what he had to say about the Bible. After the study, his friends took him out to a local all-night diner and talked until the early hours of the morning. From that point on, the Bible study became part of Johnny's weekly routine. He enjoyed hanging out with his friends. He made more friends and he was even getting pretty proficient in Scripture as well.

One day Johnny ran into his old high school friends. After a few minutes of chatting, Johnny asked if they would like to join him at the bible study that evening. They laughed and made jokes about it. Johnny wasn't really bothered by their reaction. They were only concerned with worldly things. He had found a higher calling. By the end of sophomore year, Johnny's entire social life revolved around his friends and bible studies. People outside of Bill's group really didn't interest Johnny too much, unless they wanted to join the gang at the Bible study.

Analysis of Scenario #1

In scenario #1, Bill preys on Johnny. Bill's introduction to Johnny was very natural and ordinary; it was just two guys eating at a cafeteria. The wolves' appearance and demeanor promoted the idea of spiritual wholesomeness, especially against the backdrop of the debauchery on a big university campus. In fact, Johnny thought his parents would love his new friends and be relieved to know that their son had made the right choice. Bill did not bring up doctrine or attack the Catholic Church, nor did Bill pressure Johnny to join his circle of friends. Rather the opposite happened as Bill's circle of friends joined Johnny. How Johnny acquired these friends seemed unimportant. He was lonely and needed companionship.

Step #3 – Invite the Potential Recruit to a Group Run Activity

Analysis of scenario #1, continued

When Bill and Johnny first met, Bill wanted to know where Johnny attended church. The reason Bill asked him this question was to determine, whether Johnny was already a member of his religious sect. If he answered in the negative, then Bill's answer would provide clues as to how to approach the potential recruit. No doubt Johnny's reply that he attended St. Mary Queen of Angels tipped Bill off that he was Catholic. Once Bill identified Johnny as a Catholic, the recruitment process began by plugging Johnny into Bill's social network. Johnny probably did not notice or care that every time he met a friend of Bill's they would ask him where he goes to church. Once in the group, Johnny was pressured into joining the group's indoctrination session, which operated as a Bible study.

Bible studies are not the only activities that wolves invite recruits to join. Generally, wolves will try to determine what type of activities the recruit is interested in and customize the recruitment activity. For example, if a recruit is interested in science, the wolves may encourage him to attend a church-run lecture on the relationship of the Bible and science. If music was a recruit's main interest, he or she would be invited to attend a church-run concert or a musical jam session that followed a Bible study. If the recruit had a romantic interest in a group member, the recruit would be encouraged to come to a Bible study or lecture series. The main goal is to get the recruit into the indoctrination sessions, even if the recruiter has to use non-religious bait.

Step #4 - Indoctrination

Attending an indoctrination session is the first real step toward membership. That is why all the wolves' activities up until this point has been orientated towards this goal. At these sessions, great care is given to make the best possible impression on new recruits. Members of the group are pressured to be well-groomed, polite, and engaging, not so much because it is pleasing to God (or whatever higher-power or ultimate truth the group believes in), but in order to impress (or witness) to new recruits. Just as an inviting book cover will entice a person to read a book, good appearances at indoctrination sessions will invite the new recruits to trust the session leader(s) and uncritically listen to what is said.

Appearances are not the only manipulation used in indoctrination sessions. Wolves are frequently encouraged to "love bomb" new recruits as well.

> Love Bombing - The deliberate attempt by the members of the group (often coordinated to involve the group as a whole) to shower recruits with manufactured attention or interest. The ulterior motive for "love bombing" is to emotionally manipulate recruits into embracing the group's teachings.

Everyone has an innate desire to be accepted and wanted. Love bombing during indoctrination sessions encourages the recruit to trust the members of the group and to accept what is said. Love bombing also supplies a shot of positive reinforcement that especially appeals to people who suffer from low self-esteem. In the scenario, Johnny noted how the members of the Bible study were very nice and that they were interested in what he had to say about the Bible. Through repeated positive reinforcement, Johnny began to style himself as being proficient in the Scripture. Johnny did not realize that he was becoming proficient not in Scripture, but in *how the group* interpreted the Scriptures. The positive reinforcement given at the Bible studies encouraged Johnny to continue to be indoctrinated through these studies by attaching a positive emotional value to the teachings. We will discuss this in greater detail below.

The content of the first indoctrination session will vary. The wolves will not invite a recruit to a meeting that could offend him. More or less "neutral" subjects are more effective, such as creation and science, economics, history, living a godly life, and so on. The word neutral was put in quotes because none of these sessions are truly neutral since all of these subjects are addressed from the wolves' distinctive worldview. To avoid problems, wolves will often segregate their indoctrination sessions between those geared towards indoctrinating new recruits and those for more seasoned members.

Indoctrination sessions, unlike normal church events, are insidiously disguised. All religions have some sort of formal education sessions for new members or interested parties. These sessions are for those who want to join the church, or who have recently joined the church and want to learn more. The recruits who are brought to indoctrination sessions do not know that the sessions' purpose is to induct attendees into the group. The recruits are there for other reasons. They came to the session because they wanted to hear a concert, listen to a lecture, or join a Bible study. No one said anything about becoming members.

Worldview Transformation

What is the goal of indoctrination? Indoctrination is designed not only to inculcate the beliefs or principles of the group, but also to transform the recruit's worldview into the wolves' worldview.

> Worldview: A single, coherent viewpoint or understanding of reality upon which one bases one's life and actions.

The end of Scenario #1 provided a glimpse into how Johnny's worldview had subtly changed. Before the study, Johnny's world was divided into old friends, new friends, and strangers. After the studies, Johnny's world consists only of "bible-minded" friends and those of worldly pursuits. Johnny's new worldview became apparent when he met his old high school friends. Before the indoctrination sessions, Johnny would have welcomed them and he would have fit right into the group because of their shared views and values. However, when Johnny met his old friends, he invited them to join the new center around which his entire social life revolved: the Bible study. When his old friends rejected the idea, Johnny labeled them in terms of his new worldview: they were worldly minded, and he dismissed them without further consideration.

Slowly, meeting after meeting, the recruit's perspective of the world begins to take the shape of the wolves'worldview. Since the recruit's religion is not directly attacked, he lowers his critical defenses. Eventually, he passively accepts the group's unspoken presuppositions and assumptions. The group's social network continuously reinforces the new worldview; everyone thinks the same, uses the same language, and has essentially the same perspective on almost everything.

The change in worldview happens almost imperceptibly. At the first meeting, the recruit will perceive the wolves seem to be a little odd, eccentric, or perhaps overly-enthusiastic. After the recruit adopts the wolves' worldview, the situation is reversed. Now the world seems odd, out of place, or unintelligible, while the wolves appear to be perfectly normal. From the recruit's perspective, nothing has really changed. This phenomenon is a curious thing to observe. The person changed from a devout Catholic to a rabid anti-Catholic while claiming that nothing really has changed in their lives.

Poison the Catholic Well

In addition to the positive indoctrination to the group's worldview, recruits are slowly exposed to negative reinforcement. Direct attacks against the Church are normally not made because full frontal assaults arouse the recruit's critical defenses and impede indoctrination. The last thing the wolves want is for a recruit to start thinking critically. Negative reinforcement is usually more subtle, but just as powerful; smiles disappear whenever Catholicism is mentioned; jokes are made at the Church's expense; Catholic ideas are dismissed, brushed aside, or ridiculed as silly.

As the recruit becomes a fixture within a group, the negative reinforcement will become more explicit. Group studies or lectures may be peppered with demeaning or deriding comments regarding Catholic doctrine, practice, or leadership. Individual members may begin to be more vocal in correcting Catholic doctrine. If a recruit resists this negative reinforcement or attempts to correct some misunderstanding, the group will give a thought-stopping cliché; the recruit is being "too argumentative," "going beyond the scope of the study" or "going ahead of the group."

> Thought-Stopping Cliché: A thought-stopping cliché is a verbal warning that a line of thought is going outside the boundaries of a group's worldview. The cliché is an implicit command to dismiss an idea as not worthy of further consideration.

Summary

"Love bombing," positive and negative reinforcement, suppression of critical information, and the unconscious adoption of the group's presuppositions and assumptions all combine to mold and reshape the recruit's worldview.

Mind and Body

Sheep-stealing is not merely an intellectual enterprise; it involves many different facets of human life. We are not angels, but body-soul composites. What we believe affects how we live and how we live affects what we believe. Beliefs affect every area of life. What we believe about God will shape our views on our relationship to God. Our relationship with God will affect questions on the value of human life and how we ought to be governed. Although people do not always live consistently with their beliefs, the principle remains. What we believe and what we do are intimately related.

Recruits are not immune from this unity. As the wolves' new worldview is appropriated by the recruit, the recruit's views and actions begin to change as well. At this point in the recruitment process, parents and loved ones begin to notice that something is different about their child, such as:

- slight personality changes
- changes in views on religion, politics, or some other aspect of life
- the emergence of jargon or redefined terminology
- pre-occupation or obsessions with a person, book, or topic

  These changes, especially early in the recruiting process, are not very pronounced and they are often dismissed by parents as the effects of stress or some other malady. Chapter 4 will explore in more detail the common warning signs of recruitment and how parents should respond.

Step #5 – Commitment

Since the goal of indoctrination is membership, the recruit will be pressured to make some sort of commitment to the group. Indirect pressure is used first. Recruits are made to feel odd or out of place within the group because they are not full card-carrying members. Eventually, the pressure becomes more direct and personal by plugging the recruit into the mission of the church, group, sect, or cult. For example, if a new recruit is a good singer or musician, he may be repeatedly encouraged by the recruiter to become a member so that he or she could help the music ministry. If a recruit has organizational skills, the recruiters will promise the recruit a leadership position after he or she commits to the group. The recruit's unique skill set or expertise (whether real or imaginary) is directed towards the group's mission. The recruit is sometimes made to believe that the group cannot accomplish its mission without the recruit's commitment.

Groups will sometimes manipulate a recruit into believing that he alone is the key to the success of the group's mission. By making the recruit believe that he is *the essential* piece, the recruit begins to visualize himself with the group and take ownership of the group's mission. But that is not the end of the story. Once the recruit commits to the group, he realizes that there are other missing pieces to the puzzle that need to be filled as well. Therefore, he dedicates himself to filling these missing components with new recruits. The "missing piece" manipulation may not be most common, but it illustrates the type of manipulation to which some wolves will stoop to fill their ranks.

The actual commitment differs from group to group. Commitment can be made in the form of a public ceremony such as a re-baptism ceremony or signing the membership rolls. Others use less formal signs of commitment, such as joining a public rally or demonstration, or some sort of public repudiation of the recruit's former faith.

After the recruit has made a commitment, the love-bombing and other recruitment techniques stop. The recruit-turned-new-member's attention has turned from trying to fit into the group to recruiting new members for the group.

Step #6 – Missionary Work at Home and Abroad

Missionary work is the logical consequence of commitment. Wolves do not simply allow missionary work by new members; they encourage it. Missionary work cements the recruit's new worldview by putting beliefs into action. At first, this idea may seem counter-intuitive. Does missionary work expose recruits to opposition? How can encountering opposition cement the recruit's commitment to the group's worldview?

During the recruitment process, the recruit is taught how to interpret opposition. They may have been told that all those who oppose them are somehow unenlightened, ignorant, or perhaps evil. Groups commonly reinterpret opposition by outsiders as an implicit confirmation of the truth of their worldview. For them, the truth is always opposed. Therefore, the more opposition a group member encounters, the more the member is convinced.

Scenario # 2 – Jane's Big Bomb

The family summer picnic was coming up and Jane was anxious. Unbeknownst to Jane's family, she had been successfully recruited by a co-worker and joined a sect. Jane was afraid to talk to her family about her decision because she wasn't sure she knew enough to win her family over to the truth. "If I could show them the truth," Jane hoped, "my family would see what I see and they would be enlightened too." After much study, Jane was ready to make a stand at the family picnic.

Before she left for the picnic Jane confided to her close friends what she wanted to do. They encouraged her and reminded her that her family would most likely persecute her since she had found the truth. They quoted Matthew 10:34-36: "Do not think that I have come to bring peace upon the earth. I have come to bring not peace but the sword. For I have come to set a man 'against his father, a daughter against her mother, and a daughter-in-law against her mother-in-law; and one's enemies will be those of his household;" and John 15:18-19: "If the world hates you, realize that it hated me first. If you belonged to the world, the world would love its own; but because you do not belong to the world, and I have chosen you out of the world, the world hates you." They prayed with her invoking Jesus' promise in Luke 21:14-15 that He would give her a "...wisdom in speaking that all your adversaries will be powerless to resist or refute."

At the picnic, Jane waited for a good opportunity to share "the truth" with everyone, which arrived late in the evening. Jane's mother asked her which Mass she was planning to attend the following day. Jane couldn't contain herself. She announced in a loud voice that she wasn't going to Mass and that she never intends to step foot in a Catholic Church again. Without missing a beat, Jane launched a torrent of Scripture verses and diatribes against the Church. After a few minutes, Jane ran out of ammunition and waited for a response. Her parents and the rest of the onlookers were stunned. Jane's parents lost their composure. "How dare you say such things!" they yelled. "You've been deceived! You're going to stay Catholic and that's all we are going to say about it." Flustered, Jane pulled out her Bible and began reciting all the objections that she had learned over the past couple of years. Jane's parents, being caught flatfooted and unprepared, could only retort, "The Catholic Church is true, you just need to have faith." By the evening's end, Jane's parents left the picnic sobbing and upset. Jane showed little regret for the pain that she had caused. On the contrary, she felt empowered. Jane had been persecuted for the truth just like the Scriptures said and she was convinced that God gave her wisdom that her parents were unable to refute. Now more than ever, Jane knew that she made the right choice; she was truly one of the elect.

Analysis of Scenario #2

The wolves' worldview functions as an interpretive template through which the recruit views reality. Resistance and opposition (which the wolves style as persecution) are redefined with self-serving meanings.

The idea that persecution identifies one as a true follower of Christ is simple flawed logic. If true believers are persecuted, it does not necessarily follow that all persecuted are true believer. People can be persecuted for all sorts of reasons. The statement "all true believers will be persecuted" is not the same as the statement "*only* true believers will be persecuted." The same illogic can be applied to the phrase "all dogs have tails." If all dogs have tails, it doesn't follow that all animals with tails must be dogs. Cats have tails as well. The wolves' proof that persecution identifies them as true believers is pretzel logic.

After encountering such strong opposition from parents and loved ones, most people are somewhat self-reflective. Instead, Jane's new worldview only allowed one interpretation. Opposition and resistance did not shake Jane's worldview; it strengthened it.

Step #7 – Enlist Expert Help

Parents are often at their wits' end before this next step is taken. Their child has undergone substantial indoctrination and has probably already committed to the wolf-pack. Discussions invariably turn into arguments and their child always appears to have a greater command of the subject. At this point, parents typically call an expert.

Frustrated by their child and desperate for help, parents often seek out anyone knowledgeable in theology who will meet with their child. The person can be the pastor of their Church, a director of religious education, a deacon, a religious, or an usher who seems very devout. The parents soon find that all these people, with the possible exception of the usher, are very busy. To make matters worse, their child is not terribly eager to talk to someone associated with the Church. As far as your child is concerned, he or she is right and anyone who opposes the truth is wrong. The parents finally get an appointment with an "expert," and after much cajoling, their child finally agrees to go to the meeting.

The parents have unknowingly set up a high-stakes showdown. If the meeting fails to poke some serious holes in the child's belief-system, the child will never again listen to anything a Catholic has to say. To the child's mind, he or she will have bested an "expert" from the Church. Catholicism is no longer worthy of consideration. To make matters worse, the parents have made a very serious error that has doomed the meeting to almost certain failure: They have mistaken the problem.

Out of desperation, the concerned parents have sought the help of a Catholic theologian, which would be helpful if their child was still a Catholic. At this point in the recruitment, only portions of the recruit's Catholicism are left intact. To make matters worse, religious terminology has been extensively redefined. Orthodox terms have been given different meanings and have become loaded. These loaded terms act like verbal landmines, and when mentioned provoke all sorts of positive or negative meanings and emotions. Here is how loaded words or terminology work. If a person is recruited by a group who rejects the Trinity, for example, the member will have been indoctrinated to believe that the Trinity is a demonic substitute for pure monotheism and is associated with paganism. Whenever the word Trinity is used in a discussion, the recruit immediately thinks of paganism and demons, and immediately stops listening. The word "Trinity" has become a loaded term.

Unless the parents picked an expert in their *child's* new belief system (that is someone who knows the group's worldview, beliefs, practices, jargon, history, and so on), the expert will be blindly walking through a verbal mine-field. The expert will trip over these redefined and loaded terms and inadvertently confirm the victim's misconceptions and false beliefs.

Scenario #3 – Misunderstood Henry

> Ever since Henry had announced that he had rejected the Faith as a false and demonic religious system, he had become his parent's nightmare. Everything was turned into an argument. His parents were beside themselves. They bought Henry a catechism hoping that he would read it and realize where he had gone wrong. Instead, Henry read it only to find things to complain about. When the family turned on Catholic television programs, Henry would leave the room in a huff, or nit-pick the program to death. Exhausted by constant confrontation and feeling that their son was

slipping further and further away from the Faith, Henry's parents enlisted the help of their parish priest, Father Jim. Father Jim had baptized Henry, and he was a very solid and holy priest.

Fr. Jim was the pastor of a very large church and it was difficult to find a date and time when he would be available to meet. Finally, Fr. Jim made time for a short meeting with Henry after the last Mass the next Sunday. Henry's parents were overjoyed. Fr. Jim was their knight in shining armor coming to rescue their child. Henry was considerably less enthusiastic. Nevertheless, he agreed to meet. Over the next week, Henry reviewed all his arguments and engaged the support of his like-minded friends.

Sunday arrived and Henry was prepared for battle. Fr. Jim, on the other hand, had little time to give the meeting much thought. He had known Henry's family for many years and he thought that Henry's new found infatuation with religion could be easily brushed aside. After Mass, everyone gathered in the rectory. Henry sat on one side of the table with his Bible and pile of notes and pamphlets and Fr. Jim sat at the other side. "So Henry, your parents tell me that you have some questions about the Catholic Faith." Any expectation of a friendly dialogue immediately evaporated when Henry responded with a somewhat irreverent attack on several Catholic doctrines. Fr. Jim was not flustered and he calmly refuted each of Henry's objections. Although Fr. Jim gave great explanations, Henry was supremely unsatisfied. What Fr. Jim didn't realize was that the terms he was using had been redefined for Henry to mean something very different. Therefore, Fr. Jim's great explanations were actually reaffirming Henry's new-found prejudices and fears. Henry launched more objections.

Over and over again, Fr. Jim unwittingly reaffirmed misconception after misconception. The conversation soon became heated. No matter how clearly Fr. Jim tried to explain the Catholic Faith, Henry would not understand. Finally, after explaining the same point for the third time, Fr. Jim felt that Henry was just being obstinate and was refusing to listen to reason. Time ran out just as the meeting reached a fever pitch. Fr. Jim uncharacteristically lost his cool and said, "I'm your pastor. You believe what I tell you to believe. Stop all this nonsense!"

Henry's parents apologized profusely to the holy priest for upsetting him and thanked him for taking the time to talk to their son. Henry, on the other hand, didn't have much to say. He walked away from the meeting convinced more than ever that his friends were right: Catholicism is a false religion, and any further meetings would be a waste of time.

Analysis of Scenario #3

Father Jim made one crucial mistake; he assumed that Henry was still intellectually Catholic. Henry wasn't. By not knowing Henry's new belief-system and jargon, Fr. Jim's excellent explanations were either meaningless or misunderstood by Henry. Moreover, Henry's objections were also misconstrued by Fr. Jim, since the terms that Henry used had been redefined by his new belief-system. Had Fr. Jim met Henry earlier in the recruitment process, the meeting may have gone differently.

The Lone Wolf Scenario

The seven steps outlined form the basic pattern for sheep-stealing. There are, of course, variations to this pattern. For instance, we have only discussed how a group of anti-Catholic wolves (which we called a "wolf-pack") may sheep-steal; but what about a wolf acting alone? How would the process of recruitment look for a lone wolf? Consider the following scenario.

Scenario #4 – Susan Becomes a Radical

Susan's freshman year in college had been troubling. Not knowing what her major would be, Susan decided to load up on elective courses. One course on her schedule caused her particular anxiety; Susan had signed up for an Introduction to Philosophy class even though she had never studied philosophy in high school. The textbook was intimidating and she quickly became lost when she tried to read the first chapters. Not willing to be intimidated, Susan decided to give the class a shot.

The first day of class was strange. The instructor of the course, Dr. Atheist, introduced herself proudly as an atheistic feminist lesbian. Susan wasn't sure what to make of the professor, but she figured that the class could broaden her intellectual horizons so she decided to continue, at least until the deadline for dropping classes.

At first, Dr. Atheist seemed overly assertive, but the topics were interesting. As Susan began to work through the material, she realized that women throughout history had been repressed by the "false beliefs and practices of religion," especially Catholicism. More and more, Susan's eyes opened to a whole different world. Dr. Atheist, being a well-educated and articulate individual, impressed Susan and she finshed the class with a high grade.

The next semester Susan took more courses with Dr. Atheist. Some of these courses were recommended by fellow students who also liked Dr. Atheist. One of Dr. Atheist's favorite mantras was "If you're not aware there is a problem, you are part of the problem." Eventually, Dr. Atheist's mantra began to hit home. Susan had been a content Catholic, completely unaware of how she was being repressed by her Faith. Now she could see how backwards, non-scientific, superstitious, and patriarchal Catholicism really was. By the end of her third year, Susan threw off the yoke of Catholicism and began experimenting with alternative lifestyles to free herself from the oppression of an all-powerful male god.

The campus offered a host of alternative lifestyles and support systems such as Gay and Lesbian fellowships, Eastern mysticism, and radical political groups. None of them seemed to fit Susan's needs until one day she met a student who introduced herself as a Wiccan (*i.e.,* a witch). She learned that several of Dr. Atheist's former students were Wiccans and the idea of worshiping nature as a kind of female goddess seemed interesting. Moreover, Dr. Atheist said that shocking people out of their complacency was a good way to bring about social awareness. What could be more shocking than being a witch? Susan hoped that by promoting a radically non-Christian lifestyle, she would shock Christians out of their male-dominated oppressive religion and into something more akin to what she believed.

Susan's family didn't keep very close tabs on her after she left home. Her grades were excellent and she seemed to be enjoying college. By the time her family became aware of her distinctly anti-Catholic outlook; Susan had already become a full-fledged and a fairly well known Wiccan on campus. Her parents thought the Wiccan thing was a passing phase that she would grow out of once she left college. But they were wrong. In her remaining years at college, Susan delved deeper and deeper into Wiccan folklore, magic, and fantasy. Her reputation grew so that other students would consult her on matters of spirituality and mysticism. After college, she and a few other students purchased a small occult bookstore not far off campus where Susan and her friends could help newcomers to alternative religion find true enlightenment.

Analysis of Scenario #4

Susan's misadventure did not begin with social networking leading to indoctrination, as we have already discussed. Rather, a professor took liberties with her course material and led Susan to self-indoctrinate. After her worldview had changed, Susan voluntarily chose a social network to support her newfound beliefs. Of course, as with all the previous scenarios, the wolf (Dr. Atheist) used the same parameters of indoctrination, false or misleading information, half-truths, one-sided explanations, and the suppression of information critical of the wolf's own beliefs.

Dr. Atheist did not overtly pressure Susan to join any particular group. Being a member of a faculty, such manipulation was off limits and Dr. Atheist would be reprimanded. Instead, she laid out a worldview for her students and encouraged them to commit to it by saying things like, "If you're not aware there is a problem, you are part of the problem" and "you need to shock people out of complacency to bring about social change." Once Susan adopted Dr. Atheist's ideology and decided to act, only the groups that fit this ideology would do.

The missionary stage of recruitment (steps 6 and 7) was also different in Susan's case. She became identified with the group she had chosen and purposefully decided to be conspicuous as possible about her Wiccan identity. No doubt ridicule, strange looks, and hostile words only served to drive Susan deeper into her new persona. She became known as an authority on and purveyor of Wicca. Susan had found her place in the wolf's overall mission.

Summary

The process of recruitment begins with five basic steps:

- Target a recruit
- Create a friendly relationship or rapport
- Invite to a group sponsored activity, lecture, or function
- Indoctrinate
- Encourage commitment

After some commitment is made to the group or ideology, two further steps can solidify the new worldview.

- Missionary work at home and abroad
- Meeting a religious authority

All recruiting processes essentially follow this pattern although they may differ in order and content. Now that you have a broad overview of the wolves' game plan, you have taken a real step towards developing a strategy to make the wolves' job much more difficult.

Chapter 3 – Wolf-proofing Your Kids

Now that a general outline of how wolves steal sheep has been sketched, it is time to consider how to make sheep-stealing more difficult. There are two ways the recruitment process can be interrupted. The first is when a recruit becomes aware that something underhanded is going on and breaks off contact with the wolves. The second is when a recruit becomes too difficult for a wolf to handle. If a target is taking up too much time or endangering the indoctrination of other recruits, the wolves will move on to easier prey. Therefore, wolf-proofing should give your children all the knowledge and skills needed to detect and resist any deceptive and manipulative means that the wolves might use against them.

Wolf-proofing is both knowledge and skill based. It is *not* a form of manipulation. Wolf-proofing is not driving some form of bigotry against the wolves into your young ones' psyche. Compared to instructing and developing your children's skills, instilling bigotry is easy. But being easy doesn't make a method right. Beside the fact that instilling bigotry is intellectually dishonest and morally wrong, it is a terrible strategy because it often backfires and drives your children right into the arms of the wolves. No Christian should use it.

Scenario #5- Backfiring Bigotry

Billy was a nominal Catholic whose parents used to refer to Mormonism as a "hobo religion" made up of "unstable quacks" and "know-nothings;" that was, before Billy met Melanie. Melanie was a beautiful, kind, considerate, and somewhat shy girl who worked with Billy. After a few weeks, Billy and Melanie established a friendship; which quickly bloomed into a romance. Melanie was a very private girl, and much of her time was taken up with work and church functions. When Billy asked about these church functions, he was surprised and shocked to learn that Melanie was a Mormon. She didn't seem at all like the Mormons Billy's mother had described.

Billy also met several of Melanie's Mormon friends. They didn't compare to how his parents had portrayed them. They were intelligent, kind, considerate, well-mannered, clean-cut people, not the mindless dupes Billy's parents had made them out to be. Billy continued to date Melanie, and he eventually began to attend church functions with her.

One day, Billy's mother asked about the girl Billy had been getting so serious about. Billy mentioned under his breath that Melanie was a Mormon. "What!" Billy's mother exploded. "No son of mine is going to date a Mormon." Billy became irate. "You don't know anything about Mormons! I do. Did you ever talk to a Mormon? Well, I have and they are good people! Everything you said about them was wrong! In fact, they know a lot more about religion than you." His mother was taken completely by surprise. Quickly, she tried to recall a few objections that she had heard years ago about Mormons. Billy had learned a few things at Melanie's church functions, so he had responses to these objections. It became apparent to Billy that everything his mother had said about Mormonism contradicted his own experience. Even more disturbing was the thought, "If my parents could be so wrong about the Mormons, are they wrong about other religious things as well?"

Billy dived all the more into Mormon activities until he became a fixture at Melanie's church. Eventually, Billy and Melanie broke up and went their separate ways. Billy continued to keep in contact with some of his Mormon friends, but he no longer attended any church. After Melanie, Billy's relationship with his family was never the same. The religion that once bound the family together became a source of contention.

Analysis of Scenario #5

Bigotry backfires. When gross generalizations are discovered to be just what they are - gross generalizations - a recruit has to choose between his own observations and what his parents have told him. Personal experience wins out almost every time. What's worse is that parents lose their credibility, which is a difficult thing to build and an even harder thing to reestablish once lost.

We should also note that, without realizing it, Billy had been recruited into Melanie's church through a technique known as "missionary dating."

Missionary Dating: A ploy used by young adults (and, to a lesser extent older, adults) to date people outside of their faith or belief-system for the purpose of recruitment.

In the scenario above, Melanie dated Billy even though he wasn't a Mormon in order to pull him into her church functions. Billy learned about Melanie's motives a few years later. As with most missionary dating, once the person is sufficiently inside the group, the relationship fizzles and the couple breaks up. Sometimes missionary dating results in a marriage, but a vast majority of the time it is the Catholic who has to leave the Church or get married outside of the Church.

Authentic Wolf-proofing

Authentic wolf-proofing is not preaching or lecturing to your kids. It is instilling in them the skill sets, education, and authentic Catholic worldview to enable them to discern truth from deception.

Wolf-proofing is not a one-time exercise. It needs to be made a natural part of your child's upbringing. Parents should focus their attention on the following suggestions. Each contains up to three subsections, the strategy or reasoning behind the given suggestion, practical advice for implementing the suggestion, and hints or tips on fun activities that your family may wish to do to help reinforce and integrate the suggestion into the life of the family.

The Three-cord Rope of Catechesis, Apologetics, and Evangelism

Ecclesiastes 4:12 says that a three-cord rope is not easily broken. Every Catholic child should have a combination of good catechesis, apologetics, and evangelism. These are the three cords that bind us to Christ's truth.

Catechesis

Catechesis is "...an education in the faith of children, young people and adults which includes especially the teaching of Christian doctrine imparted, generally speaking, in an organic and systematic way, with a view to initiating the hearers into the fullness of Christian life" (CCC 5).

Catechesis concerns *what* we believe as Catholics; it studies the propositional content of our faith. Catechesis answers questions such as, *Who is Jesus? Why did Jesus die on the cross? How shall we live? What are the Sacraments? What is the Resurrection?*

Strategy

When a treasury agent begins his training, he doesn't begin by studying all the various types of forgeries. Rather, the agent begins instruction by studying an authentic treasury note. By learning the details of an authentic note, the future agent will be able to spot a forgery a mile away. The same principle applies to the Faith. Through proper catechesis, Catholics learn the real thing so that the misrepresentations and distortions of Catholic doctrine are more easily identified. Good solid catechesis, therefore, makes it more difficult for wolves to reduce Catholic doctrine to a caricature without being detected.

Practice

There is an abundance of quality catechetical material available for children. Your local Catholic bookstore will be able to supply you with whatever you need. If there is no Catholic bookstore in your area, you can use the appendices of this book to find Catholic publishers who can help.

Make sure that whatever catechesis your child is receiving is faithful to the Church teaching. Some catechetical programs water down the Faith or blur the clear teachings of the Church. Such a program doesn't help anyone. Most former Catholics who are now anti-Catholics were victims of poor catechesis. You don't see the harmful effects of a watered-down or inaccurate catechetical program until children grow up and are challenged to defend their distorted catechesis. When they become adults, they realize that what they learned in catechesis really isn't very defensible or satisfying. They may think that if the distorted points of doctrine are wrong, the rest of his catechesis may also be wrong. However, the truth is preeminently defensible and Catholicism is true. Poor catechesis leaves young adults vulnerable to anti-Catholic attacks by impairing their ability to know when the Faith is being misrepresented or distorted.

Hint #1 – If your child attends a Catholic school or C.C.D. program, do not assume that the religion class alone is sufficient to catechize your child. Catechesis always needs to be reinforced at home. Take whatever book or booklet is being used, review the material, and make a comparison between what it is teaching and what is taught in the Catechism of the Catholic Church.

Hint #2 – Parents should always have a copy of the Catechism of the Catholic Church available when catechizing at home. If your children are old enough to read and have good comprehension skills, direct them to the proper paragraphs in the Catechism and have them read and explain them. By reading the Catechism, your children will benefit in two very important ways: (1) they will learn that the Catechism of the Catholic Church is the go-to source for what they need to know about Church beliefs, and (2) they will have first-hand experience of exactly what the Church teaches. For example, if a wolf attempts to persuade your child that Catholicism teaches that statues are gods that should be worshipped, your child won't have to depend upon mom and dad's word to defend Catholicism. They will have a visual memory of reading the answer in the Catechism. As we said earlier, given the choice between someone's word and one's personal experience, personal experience tends to win. Make the Catechism part of your children's personal experience.

Apologetics

Just as catechesis addresses *what* we believe, apologetics investigates *why* we believe what we do. Using logic, history, and Scripture, apologetics endeavors to provide a rational explanation or a foundation for our Catholic beliefs and practices. It also provides material to help analyze and refute opposing views. In short, apologetics is where catechesis engages an unbelieving world.

As rational creatures, we demand to understand everything we believe and do. The Catholic Faith contains supernatural truths that cannot be known through reason alone; they are revealed by God and require his grace to believe. However, how we know that these things are revealed by God, who can neither deceive nor be deceived, can be rationally demonstrated through apologetics.

Apologetics is generally broken down into three main fields:

(1) Issues concerning the existence and nature of God (Theistic Apologetics)

(2) Issues concerning the uniqueness of Christ and Christianity (Natural, or Christian Apologetics)

(3) Issues concerning the uniqueness of the Catholic Church among other Christian religious bodies (Catholic Apologetics)

A child should have a solid grounding in all three areas, especially Theistic and Catholic apologetics, since these are the current hotspots in our culture. For areas that have a large non-Christian population, Natural, or Christian Apologetics may need to be emphasized more than the other two.

Strategy

Many groups (especially coercive cults) deliberately withhold information about themselves to new recruits. They may deny, and, in some cases even lie, about incidents in their history or doctrinal changes that call into question the legitimacy of their group. Apologetics can give your child the ability to cut through the group's facade by knowing (at least generally) their true history and doctrine.

Catechesis and apologetics strengthen and enrich each other. Apologetics provides catechesis with a rational foundation and the roots upon which it is built, and catechesis provides apologetics with a well-defined system for discerning truth from falsehood and the defensible from the indefensible.

Practice

We are fortunate today to be in the midst of a rebirth of interest in apologetics among Catholics. Until five decades ago, apologetics was a common curricular component in Catholic high schools and college religion courses. In the 1960s, however, apologetics fell out of fashion, and became practically non-existent within the standard Catholic curriculum of the 1970s and 1980s. These decades also showed an exponential growth in Catholics falling victim to sheep-stealing wolves.

By the late 1980s, hundreds of thousands of Catholics had left the Church to join non-Catholic churches, groups, sects, and cults. The call was eventually made for a new catechism, a new evangelism, and, subsequently, a new apologetic movement. As a result, the average well-stocked Catholic bookstore will have plenty of good, solid apologetic material on their shelves.

Hint #1 – In a prominent area in your home, dedicate at least one bookshelf (if not a whole bookcase) to Catholic books, reference materials, and media. The bookshelf should include catechetical material, apologetic books (including at least one or two apologetic books in a Question and Answer format), and a selection of apologetic works that focus on the most prevalent anti-Catholic churches, sects, or denominations (don't forget to include at least one book on Atheism). A Catholic bookshelf creates an area in your home where you children will know to get answers when they need them. Sometimes, if someone is being recruited, they will be too embarrassed to ask others for help. The Catholic bookcase provides a non-threatening means to get answers without too much fanfare. The bookshelf idea also communicates that there are answers to problems and that they can be accessed through a little research. The Appendix titled "How to Start a Catholic Apologetic Library" will provide several recommendations on books and other media worth putting on your shelves.

Hint #2 – Teenagers and young adults love being playfully combative and apologetics is a good way to channel this natural impulse into something fruitful. Add mock-debate and play-acting to your apologetics studies. Play the anti-Catholic and throw objections at your children so that they learn to think on their feet. While play-acting, attempt to misrepresent the Faith and have them correct you. When they become more proficient in play acting, be more aggressive: change the subject when you are cornered, playfully attack them personally, and twist their words and arguments to see if they catch you. One of my most popular talks for youth groups is when I introduce myself as an Atheist or some other anti-Catholic. My talk begins with a short and pointed discourse in which I throw out all sorts of objections and then become a human piñata as they get their crack at me and attempt to corner me with counter-arguments. Afterward, I drop character to critique what they did right and what they could do better. The kids love it and chances are that your teenager will love it, too.

Evangelism

Catechesis describes *what* we believe. Apologetics describes *why* we believe. Evangelism introduces people to *who* we believe in. Evangelism is an encounter with the person and work of Christ. Without evangelism, catechesis is just words and apologetics is nothing but abstractions. Unless your child has a living, prayerful, sacramental, relationship with Christ, everything else in the Faith will ring hollow.

Strategy

Whatever grace and truth can be found in anti-Catholic groups, they do not have the fullness of Christ as we do. It's as simple as that. Outside the Church, you may find exciting worship, a deep love of the Bible, fierce convictions, a deep motivation to live a Christian life, and a real relationship with Christ. But there will always be something missing. By evangelizing your children, you give them the greatest gift a parent can give to know and love God in an intimate way. Nothing else will suffice.

Practice

How can a parent introduce his children to the person and work of Christ? Is God going to appear and perform a miracle in their life? God could, but rarely. God can be clearly seen in our lives, not only through a onetime event, but also throughout our personal histories. I believe God's work can be seen not as in an English sentence, where we read words from left to right, but in our history, where God's work can be seen from then to now. The Bible itself is a great example of my point. Scripture not only gives us the word of God, but also reveals to us what God has done in history.

God is active in the daily life of the believer. Take a few moments at the end of each day to reflect on what God has done in your life that day, that week, that month, and that year. You'll see that God has come to your aid and directed your life in more ways than you realized. Share these instances with your children. Encourage your children to be aware of God's actions in their lives, as well, and have them share these instances with the family. Teach them to respond to God's love with gratitude, thanks, and praise.

The most powerful way parents can evangelize their children is through example. Being faithful and walking the Christian walk powerfully communicates the presence of God and his work of grace in your life. Beware, though, because the opposite is also true. The worst thing you can do for your child's faith is to be a hypocrite. Parents sometimes use the possibility of failure and hypocrisy as a cop out. "Since being hypocritical is so devastating to my child," some parents reason, "I shouldn't make too much of my faith. That way I'll never be accused of being a hypocrite." Trust me nobody is more aware of the sins of a parent than his children. They know that you sin and occasionally fail to live up to God's calling. They sin and fall short, as well. What your children need is an example of someone who seeks reconciliation and forgiveness after sinning and moves on with life. Lowering standards doesn't teach this.

Evangelizing your child is easy as long as you are evangelized. Therefore, if you do not have a solid, living faith in Christ and a deep love for Him and His Church, you need to begin evangelizing yourself, too. Meet Christ, know Christ, love Christ, and talk to Christ in prayer. Your life will be transformed by his love and so will your children.

Hint #1 - Family prayer is a very natural and organic means of beginning evangelization. Gather together as a family each night. When you ask God for help and He answers your prayers, share them with your family and give thanks. Train them to thank God in prayer when their prayers are answered and to trust in God even when there is no immediate answer or if His answer appears to be "no." Share experiences when God answered "no" only to bring about a greater good that you weren't expecting.

Hint #2 - Expose your children to age-appropriate testimonies. There are many audio CDs and videos of people sharing their often painful journeys into the Catholic Faith. Such testimonies are great tools for evangelism because children benefit from positive peer models they can relate to.

Hint #3 – Yes, God may never appear to you or your child, but He did appear to others in Scripture and to the saints. Reading these accounts may be a great place to start. Try to read the lives of the saints together as a family. There are several titles that are available geared toward youngsters. Have one child read aloud a short story about a different saint each week (or each day) and then discuss the story. Ask if there are any parallels between the world the saint lived in and the one we are living. Have the children vote on their favorite saints and do something special on their favorite saints' feast days. Systematically going through the lives of the saints is not only good for evangelism, but it is also a fun way for them to learn Church history.

Catechesis, apologetics, and evangelism are at the top of our list of wolf-proofing suggestions because they are the main points that anti-Catholic wolves try to exploit when they recruit. A solid foundation in these three areas strengthens these weak points and increases the likelihood that your child will be alerted if someone tries to twist the facts.

Encourage Active Reception of Information

All good parents try to shelter their children from the sin, violence, and destruction of a fallen world, especially when their children are young. But the time will come when they will have to face the world head on. The goal of parents, then, is to prepare their children to meet this challenge when it comes. How does a parent make that transition from sheltering to letting their children live without protection in a fallen world? I would suggest that parents learn a lesson from immunology and athletics.

How do immunologists protect their patients from contracting potentially harmful viruses? They introduce into a patient's blood stream a harmless strain of a harmful virus. The patient's immune system reacts and produces the anti-bodies needed to kill the viral strain. Strengthened and prepared by the introduction of the harmless virus, the patient's immune system is ready to fight and kill the harmful strain should the patient ever come into contact with it.

Athletic programs use a similar strategy to prepare for an upcoming season. Coaches have their teams tune up in pre-season games that are of no consequence to the official record. These pre-season games help the teams iron out problems and gain confidence by competing in real game situations. Once the real season begins, the teams are ready to compete.

When your children are old enough to exhibit critical thinking skills, you may allow them to be exposed to small, harmless bits of secularism. Talk to them about a program, song, or video and help them work out for themselves what was good and bad about it and what was and what was not pleasing to God. As they mature, stronger doses can be administered. Again, don't just expose your child and walk away. Help them to think the issues through. The practice section below will provide examples of how to make this skill-building exercise fun and educational. As they gain the capacity for more complex thought, you may allow them to be exposed to a mix of media from a Catholic and a somewhat anti-Catholic worldview. When your kids are old enough to choose their own media, you will have laid the groundwork for them to critically discern fact from fiction, right from wrong, sanctity from sin.

Strategy

Wolves want Catholics to receive their anti-Catholic propaganda passively. They've learned that confronting someone with doctrine or ideology only provokes the listener's defense mechanisms (critical thinking skills) to engage. To avoid raising the sheep's defenses, wolves will often hide their indoctrination under the guise of recreation, lectures, sermons, group-activities, stories, plays, television programs (especially dramas and "reality shows"), concerts, music, and news shows.

Don't be fooled into thinking that just because a television show isn't overtly "religious" that it doesn't take a theological viewpoint or espouse a particular worldview. Sometimes shows will operate within a Catholic worldview, but often they will operate within a worldview that is antithetical, even hostile, to a Christian worldview. For example, immoral characters within a storyline may be portrayed as normal. The consequences of immorality could be ignored or suppressed. Moral actions are ridiculed and characters who behave morally are stereotyped in a negative fashion. Authority figures may pronounce judgment against religious beliefs and practices. These things are not specifically religious, but they all dictate religious ideas and values that are contrary to the Christian worldview.

One reason the culture in the United States has become so secularized and anti-Christian is that Americans have lost the ability to distinguish entertainment from propaganda. They passively watch and listen to entertaining propaganda pieces, and their worldview slowly conforms to the views of those who produce it. Critical thinking trains your children not to receive information passively but to think through whatever is presented to them.

Practice

When your kids become old enough to understand storylines, ask them questions about the cartoons or movies they just saw or the stories they just read. Who was the hero? Who was the villain? How did the hero defeat the villain? Who was your favorite character? Ask them trivia questions about the film. "Where did the hero find the secret sword to defeat the villain? Where did the villain live? What color was his house?" By asking these questions, you are training your children to engage and to think-through what they've heard, seen, or read.

Once they've mastered the basics, ask questions that help discern the message of the program, particularly how different characters were portrayed in the story. "What do you think the program (or book) was trying to teach us? Was it good for the hero to do this or that in the story? How do you think the characters felt when something bad or good happened to them? Why do you think the villain wore dark clothing and a hat? If the sound were turned off, how would you be able to know which character was the hero and which character was the villain?"

Children who have completed basic catechesis should be asked questions about how they imagine God would react to the story or a song: "Would God be pleased if everybody acted like the characters in the story? Why was a particular thing in a story or song good or bad? What would have been a better thing for the character to do?" Questions such as these can help your children engage in order to interpret from a practical and theological perspective. More advanced children can receive more detailed questions.

You may be thinking to yourself, "I watch a lot of movies, but I've never fallen prey to hidden messages." My next suggestion may be an eye-opener to you.

One fun game is to quiz each other after a movie about details in various scenes. Scenes for motion pictures are shot out of sequence. For example, the opening scene in a movie may be the last scene scheduled for shooting. After everything has been shot, all the scenes in the movie are spliced together into their proper sequence. Sometimes a director may wish to reshoot a scene. However, the set for the scene has already been torn down, so it needs to be reconstructed exactly as it was so that all the scenes in the movie have continuity. In order to ensure this continuity, every set is meticulously catalogued and the location of every object is carefully mapped out so that the set will look exactly as it did. What does all this mean for wolf-proofing? It means that every detail and every item that goes on the big screen is put there purposely *to passively convey a message to the audience about the character*. It is by no accident, therefore, that the villain's house has a crucifix, a holy picture, and a rosary. These items were placed in that scene to passively convey the message to the audience that Catholicism is the source of the character's wickedness or that it is powerless to prevent evil. Sometimes when all these seemingly trivial items are pieced together a rather surprising, and sometimes disturbing, message emerges. For example, if the villain of a movie has Catholic paraphernalia in his household and the hero has only secular or scientific paraphenalia in his household, a complex and decidedly negective message about Catholicism silently emerges. These messages, although given passively, are effective ways to shaping opinion. Each year, Madison Avenue advertising firms spend millions of dollars each year in product placements because they have the power of visual associations. If set design can affect the buying habits of soda drinkers, is there any doubt that negative Catholic associations can affect people's opinion of Catholicism or religion in general?

Hint #1 – Play trivia with your kids after watching a show or a movie. Ask them where there was specific object or action. For older kids, note religious items, phrases, and other details. Ask why they were there and why do they think the persons who made the movie put them there. Quiz your kids about details about movies or television programs they've seen. You'd be surprised by how observant they really are and by what kind of passive messages can be found in movies.

Hint #2 – While you are listening to a song on your car radio, ask your children what it is about. What emotion is the music meant to convey. Is the character mentioned in the song angry, sad, anxious, worried, or confused? Is it a good, bad, or indifferent message? Would God be pleased by the song? For older kids, show them how good love songs can be applied to our inner feeling of love for God. The desires to know God, love God, hold God, and touch God are genuine Christian feelings. Moreover, the relationship between Christ and his Church is that of a bride-groom and bride. Good love songs can mirror that love, but bad love songs (if they can be called that) with degrading sexual content don't fit with the kind of authentic love that we have for God and that spouses have for each other. Showing your older kids this distinction may teach them that authentic love (*e.g.*, a love between spouses) is nothing but an outgrowth of and participation in love for God. Sexual immorality, therefore, is a perversion of that love.

Prevent Overexposure

You should always preview all material that your children are going to be exposed to. Make sure that it is age-appropriate and fitting for them to see or hear. Don't be fooled by cartoons and children's programming. These also need to be previewed. There was a time when parents could trust that children's programming was safe. Unfortunately, that time has gone. Many of today's programs appear as harmless cartoons and kids' shows when, in fact, they carry adult themes, send mixed messages, and use derogatory stereotypes (*e.g.*, dads are buffoons, mothers are dizzy or distant, siblings are always mean, and children are the only characters who truly know what is going on). If you'd like your children to believe these stereotypes, then let them watch these programs. Don't be surprised when your children start acting out what they are watching though.

Conclusion

I have tried these techniques with my children, and they have become the most entertaining and revealing activities that we do as a family. We have reached the point that my children now become aware of subtleties that I miss. They will say things like, "When this person did such and so, that wasn't right. Was it, dad?" Remember, the goal is to train your children to actively receive and critically examine information that is presented to them and to discern whether the underlying message supports or is antagonistic to the Catholic worldview.

Promote Faith beyond Devotion

Faith is oriented toward action. Faith must be expressed in fidelity otherwise it is reduced to an abstraction, an idea that bears no relation to real life. We are called to live in accordance with the truth, and Scripture is replete with exhortations for Christians to live out what they believe:

> "Not everyone who says to me, 'Lord, Lord,' will enter the kingdom of heaven, but only the one who does the will of my Father in heaven" (Matthew 7:21).
>
> "Then the righteous will answer him and say, 'Lord, when did we see you hungry and feed you, or thirsty and give you drink? When did we see you a stranger and welcome you, or naked and clothe you? When did we see you ill or in prison, and visit you?' And the king will say to them in reply, 'Amen, I say to you, whatever you did for one of these least brothers of mine, you did for me'" (Matthew 25:37-40).
>
> "What good is it, my brothers, if someone says he has faith but does not have works? Can that faith save him? If a brother or sister has nothing to wear and has no food for the day, and one of you says to them, Go in peace, keep warm, and eat well,' but you do not give them the necessities of the

> body, what good is it? So also faith of itself, if it does not have works, is dead" (James 2:14-17).
>
> "Religion that is pure and undefiled before God and the Father is this: to care for orphans and widows in their affliction and to keep oneself unstained by the world" (James 1:27).
>
> Our first suggestion to wolf-proofing parents was to make sure your child is well grounded in the Faith through catechesis, apologetics, and evangelism. Instruction, however, only goes so far. Children need to see for themselves how living out the Catholic Faith transforms the world for the better. Insight such as this can be best seen when your family is involved in the social justice and outreach aspects of the Church.

I imagine that such a suggestion might be a bit scary for some parents, especially those who have been armchair Catholics all their lives. If you've never been a terribly engaged Catholic before, don't worry. The hints at the end of this section will give you several easy, non-threatening ways to get involved. Whatever you do, please do not skip this step. Trust me, living out your Faith will be one of the most enriching and beneficial things you've ever done for yourself and for your children.

Strategy

By stepping out of your comfort zone and being actively engaged in Catholic social action, you and your family are making a commitment to what you believe. You will be teaching your children that the Faith is not an abstraction; but that it is beneficial to all and that it is worth making sacrifices for God. Later in life, when your children are faced with a dilemma, such as whether to hold on to friends or remain Catholic, they will be more prepared to make a sacrifice, such as losing a relationship, than to reject part or all of their Faith.

Moreover, your children will learn true Christian charity that serves and loves all people because they are made in the "image and likeness of God." Mother Theresa of Calcutta is a great exemplar of authentic Catholic charity. Mother Theresa and the Sisters of Charity gave whatever aid they could to all of the poor, regardless of Faith. Thousands of Catholic organizations around the world follow that mission since it is the mission of the Church.

Nearly all wolves lack this notion of authentic Christian charity. Perhaps it is because the focus of wolves is to win as many converts as possible. Feeding the hungry and assisting the poor doesn't fit many wolves' worldview; it seems counter-intuitive to them. The wolves' idea of charity is that they will feed the hungry or assist the poor only after they've sat through an indoctrination session or joined their group. Some groups will only assist current members. The few wolf-packs who engage in charitable work without any preconditions, do so, not because it is part of their mission, but because it is commanded in Scripture, pure and simple. If the command weren't there, they would never have thought about serving the poor.

Practice

Become engaged in Catholic social justice as a family. Your family will grow closer to the Church and each other. Choose an activity that is safe, non-violent, and faithful to the teachings of the Church. Don't be shy. The object of this suggestion is to step outside your comfort zone and live the Faith. If you stick with it, you'll wonder why you've never been involved before.

Hint #1 – Have your family volunteer at a local Catholic soup kitchen or crisis pregnancy center. Most centers welcome volunteers to help feed the hungry, clean up the lunch room, or pass out infant care items. Exposure to hostility is minimal, while the benefits of seeing God's love changing people's lives are tremendous. Your family will see the poor receiving hot meals and other necessities at soup kitchens and will see crisis pregnancy centers saving the lives of the unborn children and mothers. Most crisis pregnancy centers will have a wall of photographs of the babies who have benefited from their ministries. Your family could be responsible for another picture going up on the board!

Since most charities operate on a shoestring budget, their schedules are often very tight. It is always good to call and arrange what you can do for them beforehand. If a charity does not need volunteers, call around. There are likely dozens of different types of Catholic charities operating in your area.

Hint #2 – A wonderful non-confrontational and non-violent event that your family can participate in is called a Life Chain. All you need to do is show up at a selected area, usually by a busy road or intersection, with hundreds of other people and silently stand holding signs with non-confrontational Pro-life messages such as "Life is the Answer." I have been involved in dozens of Life Chains over the years, and they've always been peaceful and prayerful. Invariably, there is a single car that will drive by and yell something inaudible out the window, but that pales in comparison the half-dozen cars that will honk their horns with approval and give the thumbs-up sign. My adopted kids love to do Life Chains and hold up signs that read, "Adoption the Loving Option." The national Life Chain website is www.LifeChain.net.

Hint #3 – Share with your children instances that happen at your workplace or within your circle of friends where remaining faithful to Christ and the Church required personal sacrifice. For example, if an anti-Catholic co-worker was belittling your Faith or trying to push you into denying one of the Church's moral teachings, tell your children about it and what you did to counteract their prodding. You might also share if you had to turn down a business or an investment opportunity because the business or investment supports causes opposed to the gospel. Let your family know. Pray for those who brought about the hardship during nightly family prayer. Ask God to bless them and change their hearts (Luke 6:29-36). When wolves offer your children lesser goods (friendships, social net, mission, new identity, approval, exciting worship, bible studies) in exchange for the greater good of being in the one true Faith, they will have your example to follow.

Hint #4 – For those who wish to take a bigger step, prayerfully consider as a family whether God is calling you to foster a needy child or adopt a baby who would otherwise have been aborted. Even if your family agrees that it is not the right time for foster care or adoption, the subject has been broached, showing your children that they should have open hearts and a willingness to follow God wherever He leads them. Don't forget to check with your spouse first before using hint #4.

Invest in your Faith

Children are less likely to trade the Faith away for another if they value it. How do children learn to do that? You guessed it. They learn to value the Faith, at least initially, from their parents. When a parent drops his kids off at Mass or a Church function and drives off to do something that is supposedly more important, what message is communicated to the children? If you want your children to be strong enough to forsake easy friendships, cheap relationships, and quick business opportunities and to follow what's right, you need to be willing to make the sacrifices necessary to become a better Catholic and a holier person. My life is a testament to this point because I am the beneficiary of two good parents.

Scenario # 6 – The Power of Fidelity

> Whenever I give a talk on how God called me to be an apologist, I begin my story by telling the audience a little bit about my parents. I grew up in a time when the Church was in upheaval; catechesis was generally poor and apologetics was practically non-existent. During my teen years, scores of friends left the church for other religions, but two examples girded me and helped me not join their exodus: my mother's consistent and unfailing devotion to evening prayers and my father falling asleep at Mass.

> My mother's dedication to prayer spoke volumes to me about the reality of the Catholic Faith. Jesus and His saints and angels were not abstract ideas, but real. My mother's love for Jesus impelled her to pray every night regardless of whether we children knew she was or not. My father gave a different but equally strong witness. At one time, he worked three part-time jobs to support our family; two of these jobs were midnight shifts. Whenever our family attended Mass, my father had to sacrifice sleep to be there with us. It would have been easy for him to stay at home and to sleep, but he was faithful, although he tended occasionally to nod off during the homily.
>
> My parent's sacrifices and devotion spoke volumes to me. I knew well their many faults and failings, but I also knew that they believed the Faith enough to make sacrifices for it. Before I learned anything about apologetics, I had several anti-Catholics approach me to pull me out of the Church. I never seriously entertained the notion of leaving because I knew through my parent's example that the Faith was too valuable to leave.

Analysis of Scenario #6

Children learn an awful lot from their parents, very little of it verbal. The powerful messages are conveyed by observing people live out a Christian life in integrity and at a personal cost.

Know the Bible Basics

Most Catholic children learn Bible stories such as Adam and Eve, Noah's Ark, Moses and the Passover, David and Goliath, King David, Solomon, Jesus' life and miracles. But if that is where your Bible literacy ends, you have a problem. The Church exhorts Catholics to be scripturally literate.

> "The Church 'forcefully and specifically exhorts all the Christian faithful...to learn the surpassing knowledge of

Jesus Christ, by frequent reading of the divine Scriptures. Ignorance of the Scriptures is ignorance of Christ" (CCC 133).

In addition to having a good grasp of the inspired text of Scripture, wolf-proofing parents ought to also make sure that their children know facts about what I call Bible Basics. These basics should cover:

- What are the books of the Bible and how do they fit chronologically?
- How was the Bible formed? What role did the Church and Sacred Tradition play in its formation?
- How do Catholic Bibles differ from non-Catholic Bibles and why do these differences exist?
- What is the relationship between Scripture and Sacred Tradition? Study the Vatican II Dogmatic Constitution on Divine Revelation, known as Dei Verbum.
- Why should Scripture be interpreted in accord with the Rule of Faith?
- Why is it important to interpret a passage in context?
- How do we know that the accounts of Jesus in the Gospels are true?

Strategy

Different kinds of wolves interpret (and misinterpret) Scripture in different ways. Quoting a text out of context is a common feature of their apologetics. They also understand Scripture through a predetermined belief system or an interpretive template. Unless a victim is aware of the presence of this interpretive template, it will appear that the Bible is teaching what the group is saying when, in fact, it isn't. For that reason, it is very important that Catholic teens understand the importance of using the Rule of Faith to interpret Scripture. Wolves such as atheists, agnostics, and self-styled skeptics, will attack the truthfulness of Gospel accounts and attempt to undermine Christianity at its roots. These wolves also approach Scripture with an interpretive template which assumes that God, miracles, and supernatural events do not exist. Covering the Bible Basics will provide a broad base of understanding in the areas that are most often attacked.

Practice

Begin your Bible Basics introduction by teaching your children Bible stories at a young age, as mentioned earlier. When they grow older, you should place these stories within the context of God's overarching plan of salvation with the emphasis on Jesus and the New Testament. By their early teens, your instruction in Catholic apologetics will likely include treating passages typically used as objections against the Catholic Faith with simple answers. Finally, when your children are old enough to understand, educate them about the Bible, how it was put together, and how to properly interpret a text. By college age, your children should have some awareness of the issues listed below in Hint #1.

Hint #1 – If you are unsure which passages are frequently attacked by atheists, the following may be good places to start:

1. The creation story of Genesis 1-2.
2. Galileo and the Church regarding the movement of the earth around the sun.
3. Noah's flood.
4. The historical reliability and veracity of the Gospels.
5. The New Testament texts that support the divinity of Christ.
6. Miracles of the New Testament.

A good book on Apologetics should cover these issues. Don't be worried if your children don't appear to retain all the facts and data concerning every topic. What is important is that they know that you have solid answers for them if they are interested, or that the answers can be found somewhere in your Catholic Resource bookshelf.

Hint #2 – Quiz your children about the Gospel readings at Mass. Ask them about details of the readings, the overall messages, and how the gospel can be applied in their lives. A short daily or weekly family Bible time may be helpful for older kids to become familiar with the Bible texts and Scripture in general.

Scenario #7 – It is Right to Remain Silent...

Greg grew up in a Catholic home, but he fell away at an early age. In his twenties, he underwent a religious renewal and joined a very large mega-church not far from his home. Greg loved studying Scripture and felt a strong desire to become involved in counter-cult missionary work with a special focus on the two largest pseudo-Christian groups in the United States: Jehovah's Witnesses and the Church of Jesus Christ of Latter-day Saints (Mormons). At the big mega-church where he worshipped, Greg met Ron, another church member who was also very interested in evangelizing the cults. Greg and Ron made a great team and they soon found themselves teaching classes in their church about the cults. Although Greg and Ron were both former Catholics, they didn't style themselves as anti-Catholic. They believed that Catholicism was in error on a number of important doctrines, but that Catholics could still be saved. Greg and Ron had no problem challenging Catholics about what they believed to be true, but they didn't actively search them out either.

One day Ron was skimming through a directory of counter-cult ministries in his area and noticed that there was a person doing counter-cult work not far from where he worked. He picked up the phone and called the man. A few minutes into the conversation, Ron was shocked to learn that the man was a convert to the Catholic Faith. He set up an appointment to meet with the man, hoping to find out why such a bright fellow would leave Protestantism for Catholicism.

The meeting didn't go the way Ron had pictured it. The man had some very good answers to Ron's main objections. He invited Ron to come back to meet with him again in a few weeks. After a few such meetings, Ron realized that he had misunderstood Catholicism. Moreover, he became aware that there were difficulties with his own faith-tradition that he had never really considered before. These difficulties bothered Ron more and more, and research didn't turn up any satisfying answers to his questions. Finally, Ron reached a point where he could not in good conscience remain where he was: he had to leave his ministry and return to the Catholic Church.

Ron informed Greg of his decision to leave. Greg didn't understand Ron's reasons for leaving, but Greg knew that Ron was a man of integrity. They both remained friends and continued to work together in evangelization after Ron's departure.

One day, a pair of Jehovah's Witnesses showed up at Greg's door. Greg invited them in for a discussion and he quickly called Ron to come over and join the discussion. In the meantime, Greg peppered the Jehovah's Witnesses with his best biblical arguments, to which the Jehovah's Witnesses responded without blinking an eye. The conversation seemed to go nowhere. Indeed, it seemed to end up in a draw; Greg had his interpretation of Scripture and Jehovah's Witnesses had theirs. Who could say whose interpretation was right? Finally, Ron arrived.

Ron's questions for the Jehovah's Witnesses were very different from Greg's questions; they were really out-of-the-box questions. For example, Ron asked the Jehovah's Witnesses how they knew Matthew wrote the Gospel According to Matthew. Who put together the books of the Bible? Why did the Jehovah's Witnesses' Old Testament exclude seven books of Scripture (called the Deuterocanon)? How do we know that the writers of the Gospels didn't lie or fabricate stories? And, if the ancient Church could be trusted with affirming which books are really the books of the Bible, why couldn't we trust that same Church witness on other doctrines, as well? Suddenly, the rather brazen and argumentative Jehovah's Witnesses became silent. They didn't have an answer for Ron's questions.

Greg was impressed, then a chilling thought occurred to him: "How would I answer these questions?" Greg didn't have an answer. "Apparently," Greg thought, "my understanding of Church history isn't really much better than the Jehovah's Witnesses' understanding." After the meeting, Greg wanted to know more about Ron's decision to become Catholic. Eventually, Greg came to the same decision Ron had come to months earlier: He needed to return to the Catholic Church.

Analysis of Scenario #7

Wolves reduce history to the level of abstraction. Historic figures aren't treated as real people living and communicating within a real community; rather, they are treated as isolated statements made within a social vacuum. These cartoonish characterizations help the wolves avoid grappling with difficult historical issues that call into question the legitimacy of their group. Their attempts to evade difficult questions, however, ultimately undermine the foundation of why Christians believe that the Gospels were truthful and the canon of Scripture is correct.

Canon of Scripture: The canon of Scripture is the authoritative list of inspired books that make up the body of Scripture for Christians.

For wolves, history is a thing to side-step and ignore. They prefer to focus their attention almost entirely on twisting the meaning of individual passages of Scripture (2 Peter 3:16). By giving your children the basic knowledge of where the Bible came from and how the witness of the early Christians guarantees for us the veracity (truthfulness), integrity, and authenticity of Scripture, you give them the ability to show the wolves that rejecting the witness of the historical Church is rejecting the only means we have of upholding the Scripture as Sacred.

Give Critical Information

Several years ago, I attended a Protestant symposium on evangelizing pseudo-Christian and non-Christian groups. One of the speakers was a member of a prominent pseudo-Christian group for twenty-five years. While a member, he began to research the group's history and doctrines and found out that he was a member of an organization that really wasn't what it presented itself to be. He left and founded an outreach to help members of his former group learn what he had learned. The man was very well-qualified. He wrote dozens of books about the group and lawyers frequently asked him to give expert testimony in court cases involving the group.

A few minutes into the talk, the man mentioned one of the most startling statistics of the symposium. He said that when a trained expert on the group talks to current members, *only about two percent* of those members will decide to leave the group. Two percent! That's only two people out of every hundred! He quickly added another amazing statistic. *Ninety-nine percent* of the non-members who are given critical information about the group *will never* join. Realizing the importance of these figures, he changed his focus. His ministry still does outreach, but now their main goal is prevention. By supplying your child with critical information about the most common wolf-packs in your area, you might provide an effective deterrent against these groups.

Strategy

Why is there a ninety-nine percent success rate through educating potential recruits? In the previous chapter, we saw how wolves attempt to create a one-sided picture of reality for the recruit. The wolf-pack is portrayed as impeccable, defectless, and invincible, while all groups outside of the wolf-pack (especially Catholicism) are painted as wallowing in spiritual darkness, ignorance, and sin. To create and sustain this false impression, information that is critical of the group and contrary evidence is avoided, down-played, suppressed, and misrepresented. By supplying potential recruits with critical information about the group *before the recruitment process begins,* you have short-circuited the wolves' ability to create their one-sided illusion of a wolf panacea. Recruits know too much about the group to join.

Practice

Since there are so many different types of wolves, it is impossible to provide your child with critical information on every group. Therefore, parents ought to research what groups are most active in their area, or if their child will be going away to a college or university they should research what groups are most active in and around campus. If you are unable to determine which groups to focus on, I suggest that you focus on the largest and most active anti-Catholic missionaries in the United States; Jehovah's Witnesses, Mormons, the New Age movement (Unity Church), and perhaps Atheism. Catholic apologetic books and CDs will supply you with all the information you need. Be sure that all the information you are giving your child is honest, accurate, and as much as possible devoid of rancor. Be fair, and, whenever possible, use documentation from the group to substantiate your assertions. By informing your child of the wolves' real history, doctrines, and history of doctrines beforehand, you are essentially blowing the wolves' cover.

Scenario # 8- Snail-Mail Versus the Wolves

My old friend Sarah called me one day with a problem. She knew that I had an apologetics ministry and thought that I could help her friend. Sarah's friend, Billy Jean, was a single mother of three who had been, more or less, confined to her trailer home raising her kids. Billy Jean wanted to learn more about God, but she didn't have the means to attend any church or go to any Bible studies.

A month earlier, a pair of Jehovah's Witnesses knocked at her door and offered to have an in-home Bible study with her. Billy Jean had already hosted a couple of studies in her house and had enjoyed it so far. Sarah told Billy Jean that she had some reservations about her new friends and asked if she could send Billy Jean some information on them. I asked Sarah whether Billy Jean would be more likely to read a book or watch a videotape. Sarah didn't know. I immediately went to my library and pulled a copy of a video documentary about Jehovah's Witnesses and a book that contained photocopies of Watchtower publications that backed up the video's claims. I got Billy Jean's address and sent her the package via Next-Day Express. I also sent Sarah copies of the video and book so that she would know how to answer any questions Billy Jean may ask.

Within a week or two, I called Sarah to find out whether Billy Jean had received my material. Sarah said that Billy Jean received my package and found it very interesting. Moreover, Billy Jean was anxious to show her friends the video and ask them questions. Sarah encouraged Billy Jean to do so. The following week, Sarah and I found out that something strange happened at Billy Jean's Bible study. Billy Jean told the missionaries that she had a video about their group and that she wanted them to watch it and answer some of the questions it raised. The missionaries said, "That's funny. We didn't know that there was material that had anything critical to say about our organization. Oh dear! We have an appointment to make in a few moments. We'll talk later." They left never to return. Sarah continued to send Billy Jean tapes and other religious materials to make up for the lost Bible study.

Analysis of Scenario #8

The scenario above illustrates the power of providing critical information. I never met Billy Jean. Indeed, I have never even spoken to her. Yet, because I was able to give her the right material *before* her recruitment process began in earnest, Sarah and I were able to make a successful intervention. Follow up was also important. We didn't just leave Billy Jean alone in her trailer waiting for another wolf to show up at her door. She still wanted to learn more about God, and Sarah was able to provide good Christian material and ongoing conversations about God.

Intervention later in the recruitment process is less cut and dry. Getting critical information into the hands of the recruit is still the goal, but the window of opportunity to get a fair hearing closes quickly. Had Billy Jean undergone further indoctrination, she would have had only a two percent chance of getting out. However, since we were able to immunize Billy Jean before her indoctrination process began in earnest, she became one of the ninety-nine percent of the people who would never join. By supplying your child with critical information during your wolf-proofing, you have dramatically increased the odds that your child will never join.

Hint #1 – Whenever possible, use primary source materials or documents from these groups. Several groups train their members to reject any critical information about the group out of hand. These members are told that these works are fabrications that were concocted by the enemies of the group. By exposing your child to primary source material from the group, your child will know that this response is baseless. Moreover, the use of primary documents will enable your child to either have a visual memory of the evidence or know where to retrieve at home.

Hint #2 – Wolves are not above lying to win converts. In fact, members are sometimes encouraged to lie under certain circumstances. They may call this permission to lie "theocratic war strategy" or "lying for the Lord" or "taqiyya." If the group you are studying uses strategic lying, be sure to include this information in your presentation to your child. Your child needs to understand that there are people who will lie to his face in order to bring him into their belief system.

Scenario #9 – Answering the Wrong Person

> One day, I dropped by my friend's home for a quick business meeting. To my surprise, he was busy entertaining two Mormon missionaries. They invited me in, and I sat quietly listening to their conversation. One of the missionaries, a young man who had converted to the Mormon Church from Judaism, waxed eloquent about how he had been chosen to work with a committee to translate the Book of Mormon into the Hebrew language. I couldn't resist the opportunity to ask a question.
>
> "The Hebrew translation you were working on," I asked "were you translating from the latest edition of the Book of Mormon or from Joseph Smith's original text? I understand there have been changes made to Joseph Smith's original version." My question seemed to take the young missionary by surprise. "Oh," he answered, "I studied the earliest copies of the Book of Mormon and spent several months carefully comparing it to later editions. I can assure you that there were very few changes from the original version, and the few that were made were grammatical corrections for the purposes of spelling and punctuation."
>
> The Mormon missionary lied. Either he didn't spend months comparing the original to current editions of the Book of Mormon or he knew about the extent of the changes that were made and chose to lie about them.

Analysis of Scenario #9

Sandra and Jerald Tanner of Utah Lighthouse Ministry counted 3,913 changes that were made to the Book of Mormon. Some of these changes were indeed grammatical, which is still problematic since Smith claimed that his original translation was done by "the power of God" (Joseph Smith's History of the Church, Vol. 1, pp. 54-55) and it was the "most correct of any book on the face of the earth" (ibid. Vol. 4, p. 461). However, a large number of these changes substantially altered the meaning of Smith's original text. Whole paragraphs were removed or inserted. People's names were changed. The meaning of various verses was changed as well.

The missionary, not willing to detract from his testimony that the Book of Mormon was true, decided to lie for the Lord and attempted to mislead my friend and me. Because we knew all this information beforehand, it didn't work.

Fact-based Knowledge of the Miraculous

The Faith is based upon the miracles, the mystery of Jesus' life, death, and resurrection is at the core of these miracles. Subsequent miracles, especially modern ones, do not impinge directly upon our Faith because our Faith is based upon what was given to us by Jesus and the Apostles. However, it does not follow that modern miracles are unimportant or have no use in evangelization. A good number of people in the United States do not believe miracles are possible.

Atheists and skeptics categorically deny the possibility of miracles since, according to them, there is no God to produce miraculous feats. Their worldview does not permit the possibility of a bona fide miracle. Moreover, people who do not call themselves atheists but who are very skeptical of anything of a religious nature also have doubts about the existence of miracles. These doubts occur because either they've never been told about genuine modern miracles or they are ignorant of the scientific rigor that is used to discern whether a genuine miracle has occurred. By introducing your children to the authentic miracles (both historical and modern), you can effectively immunize them from a materialistic, anti-miraculous worldview.

Strategy

It is imperative that your presentation of miracles be *fact-based.* Focus only on miracles that have been approved by the Church and that have been vetted for all the arguments of skeptics. Young children can learn about miracles in story form. Older children should learn about the data to support the conclusion that there are several well-known miracles. They should also learn how the Church critically investigates supposed miracles. By doing these three things, you are giving your children an extremely powerful antidote to and weapon against secularism, atheism, and agnosticism.

Practice

Learn how science and the Church determine whether an event is miraculous. Show how the investigation into possible miracles by science *and the Church* has been prosecuted with the utmost critical integrity and dispassionate resolve. Pick one or two miracles that have been sanctioned by the Church. Study the history of miracles and their religious contexts, since miracles are signs that point to a truth. If possible, study the particulars of what happened in various miracles.

Hint #1 – I highly recommend the book *The Miracles of Lourdes* (Galilee Trade, 3rd Edition, 1988) by Ruth Cranston. Cranston, a Protestant, became fascinated with the miracles of Lourdes and traveled there to write a book about them. She is very fair and respectful. The book briefly explains the history of Lourdes, saving most of its space to discuss the Medical Bureau at Lourdes, the criteria used by the doctors to determine whether a cure is beyond any medical explanation, and the criteria that the Church uses to form its decision. Cranston also relates several fascinating and awe-inspiring true stories of miraculous cures, complete with descriptions from the doctors who examined the patients before and after the miracle. As of this printing (2009), there have been 67 bona fide miracles at Lourdes. Most of the later miracles have *extensive* medical data to back up the claims.

Prayer, the Sacraments, and Holiness

I have saved the most important suggestion for last. Your family needs to live an authentic Catholic life. The Sacraments mystically unite us to Christ and implant in our heart a supernatural desire to live in the fullness of Him. Through prayer and living a holy life (sanctification) we grow by God's grace ever more deeply into union with him.

Strategy

As stated earlier, Catholics are especially oriented towards God through the Sacraments. We are united to Christ, and we desire to be ever more deeply united to him. Receiving the Sacraments, having a good prayer life, and living a holy life don't guarantee that you and your children will be invulnerable to the wiles of the wolves. Wolves promise the sheep that the pasture is greener on their side of the fence, living an authentic Catholic life makes these promises ring hollow.

Practice

Every Catholic is called to be holy. The call to holiness does not mean that you'll instantly turn into a canonizable saint, although, with God, all things are possible. The norm for most of us is a gradual step-by-step process of becoming holier and holier each day. When we sin by doing something offensive to God or not doing something we know is right, we should repair through the Sacraments of Confession and the Eucharist, receive forgiveness, and move on. As the Catechism of the Catholic Church states:

> "Parents have the first responsibility for the education of their children. They bear witness to this responsibility first

> by creating a home where tenderness, forgiveness, respect, fidelity, and disinterested service are the rule. The home is well suited for education in the virtues. This requires an apprenticeship in self-denial, sound judgment, and self-mastery -- the preconditions of all true freedom. Parents should teach their children to subordinate the 'material and instinctual dimensions to interior and spiritual ones.' Parents have a grave responsibility to give good example to their children. By knowing how to acknowledge their own failings to their children, parents will be better able to guide and correct them…." (CCC 2223).

Catholic parents are obliged to foster a life of holiness in their children. Through the Sacraments, families can grow in holiness, be reconciled to Christ in the Church together, and worship together. By providing a firm spiritual foundation for your children, you prepared them to withstand the temptations of the world. If your children do leave the Church, their holy childhood provides you with a solid hope for their return to the Faith.

Summary

Wolf-proofing is a process that involves the development of intellectual skills and spiritual strength as well as practical hands-on experience. The combination of all these suggestions creates a very strong defense against recruitment. Commonly exploited weaknesses in Catholic education and formation will no longer be available to wolves. In short, a wolf-proofed child will be very difficult to pull out of the Church.

Wolf-proofing benefits parents as much as children. It has been my experience, and I think most people and research will agree, that you don't really know something until you teach it. Wolf-proofing parents are teachers. By helping your child become better prepared to live in a fallen world, you are also helping yourself. Children aren't the only people who become victims of sheep-stealing; adults are also targeted. In wolf-proofing your child, you are arming yourself against anti-Catholic recruiters. Moreover, you will also be better prepared to help your friends and relatives if they are being recruited out of the Church.

All that being said, remember that wolf-proofing is a gift. Like all other gifts, it can be thrown away or forgotten. If your child or loved one is being recruited, the lessons that you've learned in chapters 2 and 3 will be extremely valuable, but you will still need to learn one more thing. Timing is critical for success. Parents need to know how to plan and implement a successful intervention when they learn that their children are being recruited.

Chapter 4 – What to Do If Your Child Is Being Recruited

A child's rejection of his Faith can be a nightmare. But what if the nightmare becomes a reality and it happens to you? What should you do? Your response to the bad news will determine whether your child will likely come back to the Church or leave for good. Saying or doing the wrong thing at the wrong time can drive your child away from the Church. We've already seen several examples of how that happens. Creating an effective strategy early on is the key to gaining the advantage over the anti-Catholic recruiters and creating a situation where you, not the wolves, have the greatest possibility of success.

What exactly is involved in an intervention? An intervention encourages the person being recruited to step away from the recruitment process and think clearly and critically about the new worldview that is being adopted. A good way to understand what a good intervention looks like is to picture the recruitment process as a magic show. A magician (the wolf) shows only enough evidence to the audience (the recruit) to give the illusion that something is what it really is not. The intervention process seeks to unveil the evidence that has been hidden or distorted so that the recruit sees what is really going on.

Unveiling the illusion created in the recruitment process becomes more difficult the longer the individual is in the recruitment process. Just as an audience may gain greater and greater admiration with each successful illusion the magician pulls off in a show, the wolves' pitch to the recruits will gain greater and greater credibility the longer the process continues. As in the case of the magician, it is easier to debunk one trick than several. However, there comes a tipping point where enough tricks are debunked to dissuade a gullible audience that the magician isn't really performing magic, but is deceiving them. The same is true for interventions. The earlier the intervention, the easier it is to reach the tipping point because there is less material with which to deceive the recruit.

Successful interventions are comprised of three components:

1. The intervention takes place early in the recruitment process.
2. Evidence is objectively reexamined by the recruit.
3. The recruiter's trustworthiness is discredited.

Let's examine these components in detail.

Early Intervention

Early intervention is an extremely important factor in the success of any intervention. Each indoctrination session moves your child farther and farther away from the Church and closer to commitment to the recruiter's group. It is as simple as that. Unfortunately, early intervention is fairly rare. Most parents don't realize that their child is being recruited until rather late in the recruitment process. By then, the odds are decidedly stacked against them. Parents, therefore, need to be able to detect early on whether their child is being recruited so that they can intervene at the earliest possible opportunity.

3 Steps for Early Detection

Step #1 - Foster an atmosphere of open communication with your child *and your child's closest companions.*

Most parents want an open and honest relationship with their children. But even the best relationships are not, in themselves, adequate to reveal that a child is being recruited. Children don't always tell their parents what they are doing, especially if they suspect that their parents would become needlessly alarmed. Therefore, I strongly suggest that parents also foster a good relationship with your child's closest friends. They are much more closely tied to your child's social life than you are and therefore better situated to notice subtle changes in your child's life, habits, and personality. Moreover, if your child is being recruited, these close friends and loved ones can become powerful allies for you during your intervention.

Open communication with your child and his friends allows you to keep an ear open for the distinctive warning signs of a possible recruitment.

Step #2 – Watch for Typical Warning Signs of Recruitment

Signs that indicate a possible recruitment can be:

- A sudden arrival of a new set of friends with the result of older friends are being ignored, neglected, or marginalized
- A new argumentative or confrontational disposition toward friends and loved ones over certain topics (especially Church-related)
- A preoccupation or obsession with material (books, magazines, etc.), an event (lecture series, a teacher, a self-help group, Bible study), or topic (the end of time, justification, etc.)
- A change in personality that usually tends to move from humorous, optimistic, spontaneous, good natured,

and non-aggressive toward humorless, pessimistic, preoccupied, anti-social, and confrontational.

- Radical changes in how your child views life, family, politics, alternative life-styles, and non-religious topics. For example, a child may be a huge fan of professional baseball his entire life and then suddenly, without any apparent reason, the child could care less about baseball, or perhaps politically your child was a liberal and then suddenly (without any apparent cause) your child becomes an arch-conservative, or your child turns from a solid conservative to an arch-liberal

- A drastic voluntary change in your child's sleeping habits and diet, especially sleep deprivation. The most coercive wolves try to deprive recruits of sleep and/or radically change their diet so that they will be more passive and docile during indoctrination

- The appearance of jargon or the use of common religious terminology in odd and unconventional ways

- A sudden aversion to Mass, prayer, or other devotions or devotional aspects of Catholicism

- Secretive phone calls and/or relationships. When questioned, recruits will try to deny the identity of their mysterious contact or about the subject matter they were discussing

If your child begins to exhibit more than one of these warning signs, there is some cause for concern, but don't get alarmed. There may be a perfectly reasonable explanation that has nothing to do with recruitment. The causes could range from stress at school, problems at work, or falling in love. Early detection is the key to success, but be careful not to jump to conclusions. Warning signs are just that, warning signs; they do not always indicate sheep-stealing. If warning signs are present, make careful observations, gather clues, and ask good questions to determine the root cause.

For me, the most telling warning sign is the use of jargon. Jargon doesn't come out of thin air; it is learned from someone else. Jargon is the sub-cultural lingo of a group, and religious jargon is the sub-cultural lingo of a religious group. One helpful aspect of jargon, from the parent's perspective, is that it is similar to fingerprints. Different groups use different jargon. In some groups, so much jargon is used that a member can tell simply by a member's choice of words how long they have been in the group. If your child begins using jargon or redefining common religious terms in different ways, make note of it. The jargon that is used may help you identify which group is recruiting your child.

Scenario #10 - Tale of the Shadow Wolf (Part 1)

One day I received an email from a woman named Clare who thought that her sister Nina was being recruited out of the Church. Clare had noticed that Nina suddenly developed an aversion towards the Mass. Around the same time Nina took an interest in reading the Bible. Clare asked her sister what was going on with all the changes. Nina confided in her that she no longer believed in the Trinity and other key Christian doctrines. As far as Nina was concerned, these teachings all came from paganism. Clare asked Nina point blank, "Who's teaching you these things?" "No one did," Nina answered. "I came to these conclusions on my own."

Suspicious that someone was influencing her sister, Clare racked her brain trying to connect people with her sister's new theological views. It dawned on Clare that Nina had started dating a co-worker around the time she began changing. When asked, however, Nina insisted emphatically that she had come to her convictions on her own and that no one was feeding her anti-Catholic propaganda.

A week later I met with Nina and had a friendly chat. Almost immediately, I recognized that Nina was using specialized jargon. Whenever she referred to the Third Person of the Trinity, Nina would consistently drop the article so that she would refer to *the* Holy Spirit simply as "Holy Spirit." For example, she would say things like, "I'm filled with Holy Spirit, just like you," instead of saying "I'm filled with *the* Holy Spirit, just like you."

The use of jargon showed me that Nina did not come to her convictions on her own. She picked it up from somebody. I knew that there were a few pseudo-Christian groups that spoke of the Holy Spirit in this fashion: The Way International, The Christadelphians, and Jehovah's Witnesses are among the largest of these groups. When this data was compared to the other jargon and terminology that Nina used, I knew that she was being recruited by a Jehovah's Witness.

I called Clare and told her my diagnosis. Based on everything we learned, Clare and I carefully began planning our next steps.

Analysis of Scenario #10

The scenario above illustrates the importance of careful observation. Clare had noticed an aversion to going to Mass, a preoccupation with studying the Bible, and hostility towards certain Catholic teachings. I noticed the presence of specialized jargon, and through that observation I was able to identify that Jehovah's Witnesses were definitely recruiting her.

As a side note, jargon isn't the only thing recruits pick up from their recruiters. Sometimes they pick up a peculiar pronunciation of a word, common phrases, clichés, and even hand gestures. There have been cases where a recruit changes his accent or dialect to match that of his recruiter. It is a very strange thing to be in a conversation with a person who suddenly switches talking in their normal northeast accent to one of a person who comes from the deep south. No, the person wasn't possessed. The recruit had been so exposed to certain sermons and speeches that he unwittingly started to parrot his teacher's voice. Such cases are fairly rare, but they do happen. The moral of the scenario is that things that seem to be the most inconsequential can sometimes be extremely helpful for planning an intervention.

Step #3 – Be watchful of paraphernalia that can be linked to indoctrination

Does your child possess literature that is all printed from the same publisher (*e.g.,* The Watchtower Bible and Tract Society, Free Thought Press, The Way Magazine)? Does he or she use an unusual translation of Scripture or insist on using only one particular translation (*e.g.*, The New World Translation, King James Bible)? Is your child reading a book that he wouldn't otherwise touch, such as the booklet, "Should You Believe In the Trinity?," "Dianetics," "A Course in Miracles," or "The Book of Mormon?" The presence of these materials *may* signal possible recruitment.

Also, be careful to observe the presence of any occult or unusual paraphernalia in their room, dorm room, or house, such as a Ouija board, tarot cards, grotesque or macabre incense burners, or jewelry; these are very serious warning signs and they call for immediate action.

Hint #1 – Be sure to jot down what you've observed that led you to believe that your child is being recruited. Try to make your notes as accurate and as precise as you can. In many cases, small clues are priceless.

Hint #2 – Taking a genuine positive interest in your child's life is the best way to protect a child without prying or being too inquisitive. For example, if your child mentioned that he attended a bible study last weekend, don't take a negative approach by saying something like, "A Bible study! Why are you going to a Bible study? Is it Catholic? Do you even know these people? They could be indoctrinating you!"

Rather, congratulate your child that he is interested in studying the word of God, then ask him what he studied, if he learned anything new, if there was a study guide, and so on. Be positive and interested. What you don't want to do is to become alarmed or criticize him. If it appears that your child is being recruited, stay calm and focused. Try to learn specifics about the group, such as the group's name, where they meet, the name of the leader, what study materials your child has been exposed to, and so on.

Objectively Reexamining the Evidence with the Recruit

Once you've determined that your child is being recruited, you need to plan your intervention. Remember the illustration about the magic show. The magician was only showing the audience enough to create an illusion. A successful intervention does something very similar in that it invites the recruit to step back from the indoctrination process and examine what he is learning from a different and critical perspective. In other words, the parent needs to present to their child all the things that the wolves aren't showing him. Presenting the information requires careful planning.

Take inventory of all the information or clues that you've gathered so far. See if you can piece together who is recruiting your child and what their beliefs are. If you have trouble piecing these things together, consult someone who is knowledgeable in the field of apologetics or counter-cult work, they may be helpful.

It is not always easy to identify a wolf-pack or anti-Catholic group. Some groups operate under subsidiary titles so as to avoid detection. For example, if your child came home and said that he or she had become involved with a group on campus called "The Family Federation for World Peace" or "The Women's Federation for World Peace," you probably wouldn't be too alarmed - that is, until you found out that these groups were cover names for the cult known as the Moonies.

Wolves also attempt to conceal from their new recruits their most bizarre and esoteric (and most identifiable) teachings. They prefer to spring these things on them after they've fully committed to the group. Therefore, if you think that your child is being recruited by a specific group, but seems ignorant of the group's most distinctive teachings, don't cross that group off your list. Your child may not have learned that doctrine just yet. For example, let's say that you think Mormons are recruiting your child. You've researched Mormonism on the Internet and found that they believe that God is an exalted human being with flesh and bones. When you spoke to your daughter, she said that the Heavenly Father (notice Mormon jargon) is spirit. Don't cross Mormonism off your list. The recruiters may have not broached the topic with her or they may have purposely distorted their teaching so as not to scare off a potential recruit.

Identify the Source

The recruitment process requires constant contact between the wolf and his targeted sheep. That contact can be maintained through regular group functions or individual meetings (whether it is face-to-face meetings, telephone conversations, even internet messaging and emails). What keeps the recruitment process running is the constant flow of propaganda from the wolf to the recruit. Once the contact is cut and the flow of misinformation ceases, the process stops and usually the recruit will begin to drift back to his old worldview. The effects of such an interruption can be readily seen in a rather odd phenomenon of a recruit reverting to his former self while on an extended family vacation. Once the family returns and contact with the recruiter is reestablished, the victim reverts back to his post-cult persona.

It is very important, therefore, to discern who or what is the source of your victim's misinformation. Ask yourself the following questions:

- Did your child begin a new friendship or join a new group around the time of the first warning sign?
- Is there a person you do not know with whom your child seems to be in frequent contact?

- Does your child ever mention the specific name of a person, a book, an article, magazine, website, or a historical figure in his conversations?

If you believe you have identified the recruiter, it is also important to note what kind of relationship exists between your child and the recruiter. Are they classmates? Are they dating? Are they married? Are they siblings or relatives? Different relationships pose different problems. The means by which they keep in contact can also play into your strategy as well.

Scenario #10 (continued) – The Tale of the Shadow Wolf (Part 2)

After some digging, Clare found out that Nina's co-worker had recently become a Jehovah's Witness. Bingo! We've identified the wolf. Or did we? Clare said that Nina never mentioned the co-worker's name in their conversations. Instead, Nina would mention another name, Ethan, who was spoken of as some sort of Bible expert. I asked Clare if she thought Nina was in direct contact with Ethan. "No," Clare replied, "Nina speaks of him as if he lives somewhere out of state." Who was this shadow-entity and what relationship did he have with Nina and/or Nina's co-worker? Clare and I compared notes and we discovered that something unusual was happening. Nina's co-worker, after having become a Jehovah's Witness, was now recruiting Nina probably with the help of the mysterious Ethan. Ethan was the co-worker's recruiter, and he was coaching the co-worker on how to recruit Nina. Since Ethan was out of state, there was a good chance that Nina's co-worker did not have face-to-face contact with Ethan. Chances are they kept in contact over the phone or Internet.

If our assumptions were correct, a strategy clearly presented itself to us. Because of the circuitous nature of the flow of communication among the wolves (i.e. from Ethan to the co-worker to Nina, with Nina's responses going back from Nina through the co-worker to Ethan), it could be possible to overwhelm the wolves' line of communication if Nina raised enough objections too detailed to be handled over the phone or Internet. Ethan would be faced with two prospects. He would either have to try to inadequately answer all the objections and possibly lose his recruit *and* Nina, or he could save his recruit by telling the co-worker to break off communication with Nina. Either way, Nina would be freed.

I gathered a sizable pile of photocopies from Watchtower and Awake magazines and a long list of objections and met with Nina. I showed her how the Watchtower had misquoted and misused sources. We looked at the Greek New Testament and the Greek Old Testament (called the Septuagint) and I showed her where Jesus claimed to be Jehovah God (*i.e.* Yahweh). Nina also learned how the Witnesses distort what Christians really believe along with all the biblical and historical information to back up my assertions. We also worked on some Bible Basics. We talked about how Sacred Tradition solves the problem of seemingly contrary interpretations of such matters as the Trinity, the divinity of Christ, and so on. At the end of the meeting, I gave Nina a stack of notes and photocopies for her to consider at home. Nina took the material, but she didn't let on in the least that she was moved by anything I had to say.

About a month later, I received an email from Clare. Nina was no longer meeting with her co-worker and her old personality had returned. Nina was smiling, laughing, and joking again just as she had before she met the co-worker. By the grace of God, our strategy worked. Soon after our meeting, Nina unloaded all the arguments that I gave her on her co-worker. Her co-worker, being a new recruit, apparently couldn't answer all of the material, so he, in turn, unloaded the material on Ethan, who no doubt seeing that he could lose both Nina and the co-worker, told the co-worker that Nina had been deceived by Satan and that he had to cut all contact with her. Once the contact ceased, and being buoyed by the prayers of her family, Nina returned to the Church. Thanks be to God.

Analysis of Scenario #10 (continued)

By correctly understanding who was recruiting Nina, Clare and I were able to formulate a plan and make an effective intervention. Nina's case was unusual. Most people are recruited by a single, well-seasoned veteran and the intervention is usually focused on the veteran. In Nina's case, our goal was to frustrate that guy who was pulling the strings of Nina's recruit.

The power of prayer was also very evident in Nina's case. I have no doubt that it was God's grace that enabled Clare and I to understand what was going on behind the scenes. Moreover, God's grace also enabled Nina to once again believe the supernatural truths that He has revealed about Himself. God answered Nina's family's prayers.

People are often afraid of anti-Catholic wolves. To be sure, wolves shouldn't ever be underestimated. However, there is one thing that you need to understand about wolves: most of them will only fight for a sheep as long as there is a reasonable chance of success. Once it becomes apparent that a sheep is not going to go quietly along, wolves will generally cut and run.

Scenario # 11 – An Unexpected Monkey Wrench

A small group of Catholics hosted a discussion group with their friendly neighborhood anti-Catholic missionaries. The group met to discuss the differences between Catholicism and the wolves' "Bible Christianity." After four or five meetings, the group grew from four people to about twenty-five people. One meeting the anti-Catholics invited a "ringer" (i.e. an expert evangelist) who kept railroading their discussion. Frustrated, the Catholic side invited me to sit in to counter the "ringer."

I didn't say anything during the first meeting; I just wanted to observe. It soon became obvious that everyone was talking past each other. I suggested that the next meeting should begin with one person from each side giving a five-minute presentation explaining how their group understands a given doctrine. That way, I explained, we can understand each other's position at the outset and we won't be talking past each other. The anti-Catholics agreed and my group nominated me to give the presentation, no surprise there.

A month later we met. The anti-Catholics expected to see the Catholic presentation tripping over loaded terminology and inadvertently affirming their misconceptions about the Church. Instead, my presentation explained the Catholic Church teaching on the given subject using the group's jargon and pet biblical passages. Needless to say, the anti-Catholic side was beside themselves. Apparently, the leader of the anti-Catholic side, a former Catholic, invited three Catholic girls that he and his friends were recruiting to come to the meeting. They wanted the girls to hear, from the proverbial horse's mouth, how Catholicism contradicted the Bible. My presentation showed the girls that not only does Catholicism *not* contradict the Bible, but that the anti-Catholic leaders had seriously misunderstood what the Catholic Church really taught.

The next meeting was noticeably smaller. Only a few anti-Catholics showed up. A week before the next meeting, I received a phone call from the leader of the anti-Catholic side. He told me that he and his friends couldn't attend any more meetings because it was "destroying their spiritual life." I told him that I was sorry to hear about his decision and that I would pray for them. But not all of the anti-Catholics felt the same way. The ringer that had been invited by the anti-Catholic side remained and eventually he ceased to oppose Catholicism. In fact, he became a good friend of mine and several other members of the group as well.

I'm not sure what happened to the three girls. The fact that the wolves' strategy backfired may have helped them see that the wolves' really weren't telling them the truth about Catholicism. Perhaps, by God's grace, they came back home.

Analysis of Scenario #11

The scenario above shows the tenacity of wolves. When there is a perceived advantage and a potential to win converts, the numbers grew. When the advantage was lost, the wolves disappeared. The scenario also shows that not all who oppose Catholicism are wolves. The "expert" for the anti-Catholic side wasn't there to win converts *per se* but to discuss Scripture. He had a lot of his misconceptions about Catholicism cleared up at these meetings and he helped clear up misconceptions for us Catholics as well. Although we still disagree on some serious issues, we see each other as dear brothers in Christ.

What if your child is near the end of the recruitment process?

The longer a person is in the recruitment process the longer the intervention will take, generally speaking. There may come a time where a recruit will refuse to look at any information or they may not be physically able to meet with you. Keep this end point in mind when you are deciding how long or intensive your intervention will be. If it is foreseeable that you'll be able to meet several times with your child, then you can work slower through the material. If only one meeting is possible, you'll need to make that meeting count.

Scenario # 12 – The End Was Too Near

Several years ago, I received an unexpected phone call from a frantic housewife. She had called the local seminary for help and they referred her to me. She explained that several months ago her husband had become infatuated with a group that believed in a series of prophecies foretelling that the United States was going to be destroyed by a catastrophic flood. According to the group, only their compound, somewhere out in a desolate area in the Northwest, would survive the flood. She implored me to meet with him before he did something crazy and I readily agreed. I took down as much information as she had and told her that I'd make a trip to the library that evening and research the beliefs of the cult so that I could meet with her husband in a few days.

That night, I received another phone call from the woman. She told me that she was nosing through her husband's desk trying to get more information and she found a one-way ticket that he had purchased to an airport near the group's compound. The date on the ticket was for the following evening. She also discovered that her husband was planning on cashing out all the family's savings as well. Apparently, the flood date that this group was prophesying was approaching and this person was going to abandon his family, take their money, and fly out to the group's compound. The intervention needed to happen immediately, and the wife had to do it.

The intervention was going to have a confrontational aspect to it, as the wife would have to admit nosing through her husband's personal effects. The chances of a successful intervention under these conditions were practically zero. For that reason, I told her that she should first make sure that her family was protected. She needed to secure her family's money and make provisions so that whatever happens with her husband they will be okay. We also talked about what I had found out about the cult, and I gave her pointers on what to say. I told her that I'd have my phone close by in case she needed last-minute advice or wanted me to come over.

Unfortunately, time had run out. The husband skipped town the next day, but, thanks to the quick actions of his wife, he left town without the family's money. The doomsday clock apparently was too close to midnight to make any effective intervention possible.

Analysis of Scenario #12

At the beginning of the scenario, our expectation was that I would have a series of meetings with the woman's husband. Because of the nature of the cult, however those plans had to be scrapped. The only thing possible was to counsel the wife over the phone and make one abrupt, messy intervention. Given how late the intervention happened in the recruitment process, I doubt that anything the wife could have said (or anyone could have said) at that point would have changed the course of events. However, seeds were planted and the wife could walk away from the episode knowing that she did all that she could have done.

Although sometimes seed planting may seem futile, as in the scenario above, you should never discount the power of God to bring those seeds to maturity and lead someone back home to the Church.

Scenario #13 – Late- Blooming Seeds

> Heather was a Catholic who loved apologetics. A family that she knew had a child who became a Mormon. He was leaving town soon so she was going to make an intervention, she was only going to have one shot.
>
> During the intervention, Heather asked the young man a question. The Book of Mormon claims that somewhere in the neighborhood of two hundred and fifty thousand Nephite soldiers were slain in battle at the Hill Cumorah (Mormon 6:1-15). Why haven't there been any swords, shields, or other accouterments of war discovered in that area? The young man gave a quick response and the conversation continued down a different line of thought. The discussion ended amiably. The young man testified to Heather that he still believed Joseph Smith was a prophet. The intervention ended without much hope of success.
>
> A few years later, Heather ran into the young man on the street and he was overjoyed to see her. The man told Heather that he decided to leave Mormonism and that her question

about the missing weapons had always stuck in the back of his mind. When other problems began to surface, he realized that the Book of Mormon was a fraud.

Analysis of Scenario #13

Not all one-time encounters are ineffective. The main task in these short encounters is to plant the seeds and pray to God that He will continue the growth (1 Cor. 3:6-7).

Your Final Approach

If your child is being recruited, chances are there will be some emotional attachment to the wolf-pack, depending on how far along your child is in the recruitment process. Emotional attachment is best defined through an illustration.

Picture a boy who just went out and purchased his first car. The car he picked was sporty and flashy, but under the hood it was a pile of junk. The used car salesman sold the boy on all the good features of the car and conveniently forgot to point out the bad features as well. The boy fell in love with his first major purchase and drove his new used car to his parents' home thinking that they'd see all the great things about the car that he did. The boy's parents weren't impressed. They pointed out that the car had bald tires, bad shocks, and it was burning oil. The boy became hurt and angry and refused to listen thinking to himself. "What do they know about cars! They're just trying to be mean."

The boy in this story was emotionally attached to his car and there was nothing anyone could say to make him feel differently about his choice, even if what was said was true. The boy's emotional attachment to the car was closely tied to the fact that buying the car was *his personal decision*. Therefore, to criticize the car, even if the criticism was factually based, was to attack the boy personally and make him feel hurt and angry. Recruits sometimes feel the same way about their commitment to the wolf-pack. It was *their* decision to leave the Church and join the wolf-pack. Therefore, when a recruit is emotionally attached to a wolf-pack, the details about the group itself are secondary to the idea that it was the recruit's own personal decision.

Be aware of this mentality when you are intervening with your child. Emotional attachment, once identified, is easy to overcome. Simply think about how the parents could have avoided offending their child and still get their point across. The first thing the parents should have done was to have affirmed all the good qualities about the car and give some sort of recognition as to why they could see why the boy chose the car in the first place. They could have said, "I see why you liked the car. It looks great and it is really sporty." The second thing they could have done was come alongside the child, so to speak, and ask him questions about whether or not he had considered addressing the negatives of the car. They could have said, "Did you notice that the car was burning oil when you drove it over here? How expensive do you think it would be to fix that?" Eventually the parents' questions would make the boy reconsider whether the car really was as good as the salesman made it out to be. The same thing can be done during your intervention.

Chapter 5 will investigate a few apologetic postures like the one mentioned above. These postures, when done well, can be effective ways to gain a fair hearing from your child while at the same time avoid conflict, arguments, and hurt feelings.

The Importance of Prayer

Before and after (and if possible during) your intervention, pray. Pray that God will direct your speech and open your ears and your child's ears to hear whatever necessary. Pray for the grace of conversion. Pray that God will take whatever seeds you've imperfectly planted and bring them to fruition. Pray also that whatever the outcome, you'll be given the grace to accept His will.

All Things Work Together for Good (Romans 8:28)

Apologetics is filled with joy and heartbreak. The greatest joy is seeing someone who never had faith become a believer. It's akin, I suppose, to watching Lazarus rise from the tomb, or to share in the joy of the prodigal son's father who said, "But now we must celebrate and rejoice, because your brother was dead and has come to life again; he was lost and has been found'" (Luke 15:32). The deepest of all heartbreaks comes from speaking with good and godly parents who lost their children through the deception of some anti-Catholics. Such misery provokes the believer to ask why God would allow adversity to plague seemingly good people.

St. Augustine perhaps had the best answer to such a question. God is so strong, Augustine taught, that He can bring good even out of evil. On the surface, Augustine's answer isn't terribly comforting. But I believe it to be true. Sometimes God allows bad things to happen in order to bring about a greater good that would not have otherwise come about. I've seen Augustine's answer lived out time and again throughout my years doing apostolate. I've seen individuals and entire families utterly transformed and spiritually renewed as a result of their child leaving the Church, even when the child does not return.

Scenario # 14- God's Unexpected Gift

> My friend Thomas is a solid Catholic apologist who had built a good reputation within his parish. One day, his pastor phoned him with a problem. "Thomas, I have someone that I'd like you to meet," the pastor said. "The other day I received a phone call from a worried husband who said that his wife, Sally, was thinking about leaving the Catholic Church and she wants to pull her kids out of the C.C.D. program." After a few minutes of discussion, Thomas knew which group was behind Sally's sudden abandonment of the Faith; it was a nearby Fundamentalist church that had been targeting parishioners in the area. Thomas called the husband and set up a meeting with Sally.

At the first meeting, Thomas noticed a large pile of familiar anti-Catholic booklets and tracts next to Sally's Bible in the front room. They ate dinner and afterwards, as Sally's husband cleaned up and put the kids to bed, Thomas and Sally chatted in the living room. "I know all these tracts," Thomas said as he thumbed through the pile. "I have copies of them at home. In fact, I thought that they might have some good points so I looked into their claims. And do you know what I found?" Sally shrugged. "No, what did you find?" "I found that they were quoting passages from the Bible out of context and twisting their meaning. On top of that, they also misrepresented Catholic teaching." Sally was intrigued and asked, "Where do they misquote the Bible?" For the next two hours, Thomas went through four or five tracts and showed Sally what he had found. Thomas also had a copy of the Catechism of the Catholic Church and was able to show Sally exactly where the tracts distorted Catholic teaching. Sally was impressed. It was getting late and Sally had a lot of questions that she wanted to ask Thomas. They agreed to meet again. The meetings became a weekly routine at Sally's house. Slowly but surely, Sally realized that her new Fundamentalist friends weren't telling her the whole story about the Catholic Church. Moreover, she found Thomas' explanations very compelling. One night, Sally confided to Thomas that she had decided to come back to the Church. In fact, she was more excited than ever about her Faith.

Several weeks after Thomas' last meeting with Sally, he received a phone call. It was his pastor. The pastor had just got off the phone with Sally, who was asking about doing some volunteer work for the church. Sally told her pastor how overjoyed she was to be back in the Church and she related a very interesting side-story about her return. After Thomas' last meeting, Sally went to bed and her husband unexpectedly gave her a kiss. "What was that for?" Sally asked. Her husband replied, "'I wanted to thank you for following your convictions and trying to leave the Church."

Sally asked, "What do you mean?" Her husband replied, "For the past few weeks, I was listening to your conversations from the other room. If you hadn't tried to leave the Church, you never would have met with Thomas and I would never have learned all the awesome things about the Faith." Sally told the pastor that her husband was as "on fire" as she was and he also wanted to become more involved in the parish as well. Thomas was stunned. Sally's husband didn't seem to be the least bit interested in the Faith. In fact, the only reason he seemed to be upset about Sally's intention to leave was that she was upsetting the status quo of the family. As a result of Sally's decision to leave the Church, her husband's faith-life was renewed and their marriage, now strengthened by a common Faith, became stronger than ever.

Analysis of Scenario #14

Sally's husband never figured into Thomas' plans. He was a bystander. Thomas' focus was on helping Sally. However, God had a better plan. At first, things looked pretty bad. Sally was leaving the Church and taking her kids with her. But out of this evil, God produced a greater good. Both Sally and her husband's faith has been renewed and invigorated.

Scenario #15 – Meet the Real McCoys

The McCoy family was a typical Irish Catholic family until the oldest son Mark began to go through some major changes. Mark didn't have a lot of friends except for his best friend Dave. Mark and Dave were inseparable. Dave began to notice that Mark had become somewhat moody lately, spending most of his spare time in his room on the computer. For some reason, Mark didn't seem to be his old self. At first, these changes were thought to be the result of taking a full load of classes at the local college. But the changes seemed to persist even when school was out. Mark had always been a fun "life of the party" sort of guy. Now, his free time was spent reading the Bible and surfing the

Internet. Moreover, Mark and Dave used to see everything eye-to-eye, from sports to politics, but suddenly it seemed like they couldn't agree on anything, especially religion.

Mark became more and more hostile toward the Church. His family found out that he had stopped going to Mass and was attending a nearby non-Catholic study group. Mark's father wanted to throw Mark out of the house, but his wife stopped him. She thought that it would be better to just love and accept Mark as he was, hoping that he would eventually come back to his senses. The strategy backfired. Mark used the temporary peace in the house to evangelize the rest of his siblings. As a result of this, the father kicked his son out of the house.

Mark's mother was beside herself. She frantically worked out an uneasy truce between her son and her husband. Mark was allowed to live at his family's house until he graduated the following year on the condition that he not to discuss anything pertaining to religion with family members.

Mark's parents didn't give up on their son. They began to listen to Catholic radio and watch Catholic shows on the television. As a family, they studied the Catechism and Catholic apologetics and became devout Catholics. The McCoys began praying their rosaries nightly together, and attending Eucharistic adoration, and praying novenas. The McCoy family was transformed. Despite the family's remarkable growth in holiness and education, as well as having innumerable talks with their son, Mark remained outside the Church. The pain of Mark's opposition to the Church is still a cross that his parents bear, but their newfound faith and devotion has helped them bear that cross. Indeed, the McCoy family has begun to do volunteer work to help other families whose children have left the Faith.

Analysis of Scenario #15

God is so powerful that He is able to bring good even out of a bad situation. Exactly what wolf was driving Mark into his new anti-Catholic person still remains a mystery and still Mark remains out of the Church, but his family grew in grace and holiness to a remarkable degree. Their love for Christ and His Church blossomed as did their confidence that their son's destiny is in the hands of the great and merciful God. God has given them the grace of forbearance and patient endurance.

Faith is a gift from God given by His grace. Arguments and answering objections may satisfy the intellect, but ultimately it is up to God's grace and the person's cooperation with His grace that makes the difference. In a mysterious way, even though God could convert a person through an extraordinary grace (as He did with St. Paul), God calls all of us to share in the ministry of reconciliation by offering solid demonstrations of our Faith, most especially through our suffrages and prayers, which are themselves products of God's grace.

Even when all seems lost God can still bring good out of evil. The two scenarios above are typical of literally dozens of examples that I could have given to show this point. Take heart, be confident, and pray.

Summary

Parents should be observant and aware of tell-tale signs that someone is pulling their child out of the Faith. The quicker you can intervene in the process of recruitment the better your chances for success. But never rush into an intervention blindly. You need first to assess the circumstances that surround the sheep-stealing. You need to identify the group recruiting him and know the group's beliefs, practices, and jargon. You also need to be familiar with how typically the recruitment process works and the transformation that occurs in the recruit. Using the information that you've put together, map out a strategy to bring your child back.

Appendix A will provide contact information of Catholic and non-Catholic apologists and ministries that can provide help and support for your intervention. Some apologists, depending on availability and whether or not they know the recruiter's belief-system well, are willing to do the intervention for you. If this option is available, it may be your best option, especially if the apologist is experienced in talking to members of your child's group. Research your topic well and present information that is critical of the group. You should have the documentation to back up this information and present it accurately and fairly. Invite your child to study the group's teachings with you.

Prayer is important throughout your endeavor to rescue your child. Conversion doesn't come about solely through arguments and information; it comes through God's divine grace and one's free will. There is also an element of spiritual warfare. Place yourself and your child in the hands of the loving God and pray. Remember, "...all things work for good for those who love God, who are called according to his purpose." God can bring about good even out of bad situations.

If there is one element upon which the whole intervention swings, it is the ability to gain a fair-hearing. In the next chapter, we will explore how best to direct your conversation so as to gain such a hearing.

Chapter 5 – What to Do If Your Child Has Already Left

Strictly speaking, wolf-proofing is a preventive measure. That doesn't mean, however, that the principles so far learned cannot be applied to children who have already left the Church only that there are additional difficulties that need to be overcome. In this chapter, we will explore what to do if your child has already left the Church, how to diagnose your situation, and how to implement a strategy to help reach out to your loved one.

Diagnosis

The first question to answer is whether or not your child was recruited out of the Church. The process of recruitment has already been examined in detail. However, the issue of how to reach out to those who left the Church without an external influence has yet to be addressed.

Rescuing those who were victims of sheep-stealing is a task quite different from reaching out to those who left for their own reason. Victims of sheep-stealing were manipulated into rejecting the Faith that they loved. These victims can be rescued by addressing what they've been given in the indoctrination process. Those who left the

Church without the direct influence of a specific group or person generally leave for other reasons.

What To Do If Your Child Falls Away from the Faith

In your diagnoses of the situation, you need to discern what caused your child's move out of the Church. There are innumerable issues that cause someone to leave, from acquiescing to a corrosive culture to being tripped by an altar boy after Mass. To simplify things, let's examine the most common categories of reasons people leave the fold.

Apathy or Indifference

Many people simply fall away from their religion. They simply do not see any real significance in practicing any religious faith whatsoever. The apathetic and indifferent often equate their religion with culture. For example, they will say things like, "I go to Church because that's what Catholics do." Sadly, for these people, missing Mass is not any worse than not drinking green beer on St. Patrick's Day.

Apathy is one of the most difficult problems with which to deal. There is a kind of spiritual inertia that needs to be overcome. In a way, a belligerent anti-Catholic is often much easier to talk to than an apathetic former-Catholic. A belligerent anti-Catholic is zealous because he or she believes that there is objective truth worth fighting for while an apathetic person isn't motivated by truth unless it affects them personally. I saw a pro-life bumper-sticker today that takes aim at that kind of mentality. It read, "Abortion isn't that important because you are not the one being killed." There is a lot of truth in that.

How can a parent help a child who is apathetic or indifferent? Basic catechesis will be very helpful. People often become apathetic when their understanding of Catholicism is so blurred, ill-defined, or watered down that they really see no difference between the Church and any other belief system. To be that obtuse, they probably aren't very clear on other belief systems, either. Catechesis and apologetics will help clarify exactly what Catholicism is and is not and bring to light its importance. If your child is already well catechized (which is possible although not likely), he or she may need to be evangelized.

Hint #1 - Sharing of good, solid, Catholic resources (CD's, Mp3, Books, Magazines, Websites, Videos, DVDs, et al.) can help. Find out what format works best for your child and give them a variety of material. (Don't forget to listen to them first just in case he or she asks questions about the subject matter). Follow up with them. Ask them what they thought. When you give away material to anyone, make sure that it is something new and of value. Why does it have to be new? Think about it. If you received something from a friend that you weren't terribly interested in, what would you do with it? If it were cheap, you'd probably toss it in the trash or throw it somewhere out of the way. Brand new items are more difficult to toss in the trash. At the very least, they will be put into a drawer or cabinet somewhere. As long as they hold on to it, there is always the chance that on some rainy day they may take a look at it. With prayer and patience, God will provide the opportunity.

After you've done everything that you can do, continue praying. Religion often seems unimportant to young adults because they believe that they have everything in their life under control. When something serious happens, the importance of religion will immediately come into focus.

Intellectual Obstacles

Misunderstandings, wrong information, and poor reasoning can sometimes become an intellectual obstacle to the Faith. Intellectual obstacles are rare in cases where a child has left the Church without being recruited, but it is possible.

Removing intellectual obstacles falls within the realm of apologetics. Don't be fooled, however, into thinking that your task is simply to answer objections. If your child has already decided to leave the Church, chances are that there are a number of interrelated objections that need to be dealt with. One very important skill that every person who studies apologetics should learn is how to properly diagnose what is a person's root problem or obstacle.

Scenario #16 – The Case of the Anti-Papist Who Wasn't

I received an email from a man named John who had some questions about the Catholic Church. John was befuddled. Every time he tried to have a discussion with a Catholic on his questions, the Catholic would become angry and tell him to get lost. The funny thing is that John wasn't anti-Catholic. In fact, he really didn't even oppose Catholicism *per se*. John just wanted answers to his questions. I wrote him back saying, "Fire away!"

John sent me a lengthy email that centered mainly on objections against papal authority, the doctrine of Papal Infallibility, and apostolic succession. At first, I thought to myself, "This doesn't seem to really be a big deal. These are pretty standard objections. I wonder why other Catholics had a difficult time with John." But there was something strange about John's email. At first, I couldn't quite put my finger on it. I read it again. John's questions were nothing out of the ordinary, but the text surrounding the questions was a bit odd, especially his description of Jesus and the Apostles. The way John phrased his description suggested that he believed that each of the twelve Apostles had their own personal (and possibly contradictory) understanding of the identity of Jesus and what He taught. After my third reading, I saw the problem. John's problem wasn't with the papacy or apostolic succession. John's problem was that he didn't think *anyone* could know *anything* for certain. John's root problem was how we know. The objections about the papacy and succession were the result of a faulty understanding of how we can know things as they truly are. No wonder Catholics became frustrated with him. They must have gone around and around in circles talking about history and Scripture when John denied that anyone could know history or Scripture with any certainty.

I asked John in my reply about what he believed about knowing objective truth and whether we can trust our senses. My suspicions were confirmed. We put aside his questions about Catholicism and focused on questions of how we know and certitude. Once those issues were addressed, John's questions on Catholicism disappeared.

Analysis of Scenario #16

There is a structure to what we know. Certain truths are based upon more fundamental truths. You can picture the structure of knowledge as an inverted pyramid. At the bottom of the inverted pyramid there are a few very important truths such as the trustworthiness of our senses, the existence of God, and so on. These issues are treated in Theistic Apologetics. These truths are the basis upon which we can recognize other truths such as the possibility of God's revelation, and the uniqueness and validity of Christianity. These issues make up the mid-section of the inverted pyramid normally and they are treated in Natural or Christian Apologetics. The largest and top-most section of the inverted pyramid contains issues concerning the Church. These issues are included in Catholic apologetics. The Catholics who had dialogued with John before I did were dealing with his issues on the top level of the pyramid (*i.e.*, Catholic apologetics) when the root cause of his problems was located at the bottom of the inverted pyramid (*i.e.*, can we trust our senses?). John's difficulties with Catholicism were the symptoms, not the cause, of John's problem.

When attempting to remove intellectual obstacles, listen carefully to what the person says. Try to determine what intellectual obstacles are causing problems, and, most of all, what is the root cause or causes. Unless you do, you may be attempting to cure a malady by treating the symptoms while ignoring the root cause or causes. Careful listening and questioning is imperative. Otherwise, your conversations will go around and around, become heated and likely end in a shouting match. When you have identified the root intellectual obstacle, research the problem and/or consult people who may know the answers and share them with your child.

Be warned. Root causes are not always intellectual obstacles. For those who left the Church without being recruited, the root cause or causes are almost always moral.

Moral Obstacles

What is a moral obstacle? A moral obstacle is the reticence or resistance of the will to live out what is true and authentic. There are many causes of moral obstacles. Sometimes a person habitually commits a certain sin. The person knows that the sin is wrong and he has begun to despair that God's grace can help him. To calm his or her troubled conscience, the person rationalizes his or her sin away by producing some sort of rational justification for their actions. The sin is no longer the individual's fault, but the Church's fault, or Jesus' fault, or God had mistakenly taught that sin is indeed a sin. In these cases, the root moral obstacles will put up dozens of intellectual obstacles as a subterfuge for the real problem.

Moral obstacles are also caused through the sins of others. A person may have been harmed physically, spiritually, emotionally, or psychologically by another Catholic or by a group of Catholics. There are many varieties of this type of injury. Whether the injury is real or perceived, the injured person has become hurt, angered, or feels rejected.

How does one remove moral obstacles? Moral obstacles are not intellectually based. Therefore, no amount of argument will remove them. Indeed, arguing will only make matters worse. Moral obstacles need to be healed more than removed. Prayer, living a holy life, and loving the hurt person with genuine Christian love is the best way to heal moral obstacles. Information and clarity may help alleviate some of the sting of moral obstacles. For example, sometimes it is easier to refrain from a sin when one knows why the sin is truly harmful, or displeasing to God. Likewise, sometimes forgiving someone can be made easier when you have a better understanding as to why that person harmed you.

Some moral obstacles are caused by fear of the unknown. A good example of fear-induced moral obstacles can be seen in cases dealing with the morality of artificial contraceptives. For example, a person may refuse to give the assent of faith to the Church's teaching against artificial contraceptives because of the fear that the alternative, Natural Family Planning (NFP), is ineffective. In these cases, considering the research, which has shown NFP to be more reliable than artificial contraceptives, can alleviate these fears. Talking to Catholics who use NFP successfully may also help eliminate unwarranted fears as well. Information, in this case, did not remove the obstacle *per se*, but it did alleviate the fear that made the moral obstacle so tenacious.

Each of these different types of obstacles requires a different approach. Some obstacles stem from a deficiency in catechesis, apologetics, and/or evangelism. Others are intellectually based, while others are emotionally based. Once you've identified potential deficiencies and obstacles, proceed to remedy whatever is lacking.

For additional help, you may want to skip the next section, which deals with interventions with children who have already been pulled out of the Church, and read the section on Apologetic Postures. Choosing the correct Apologetic Posture may serve to open up the lines of communication between yourself and your child.

What to do if your child has already been recruited out of the Church

If your child has already left the Church, many of the perimeters that have so far been addressed in this book will need to be changed. In your situation, for example, the recruitment process has already been completed and your child's worldview is essentially that of the wolf-pack. Your child's language and personality has probably undergone a change. Religious terms no longer hold the same meanings. Your child's system of communication is likely filled with loaded terms, thought stopping clichés, and he or she fluently uses the wolf-pack's jargon. Your child may or may not have done missionary work. Their life may have already grown around the group. For example, they may be dating or have married someone from the wolf-pack. Maybe your grandchildren are involved in the child's group. You may have a history of interventions with your child which have failed and may have caused damage to your relationship. When all of these factors are taken into account, your task may seem no more difficult than Joshua storming the gates of Jericho by himself. You are going to need God's help.

In previous chapters we discussed how to use observation to gather information, research the wolves' doctrines, practice, and jargon, and lastly, to plan an intervention and implement it. You will need to follow these steps. In the last section of this chapter, we discussed identifying root causes. If you've skipped that section, you may want to review what was discussed under Intellectual Obstacles and Moral Obstacles. You may find the advice there to be helpful.

There is one factor on your side. Since your child is done with the recruitment process, time is not a big factor. You have the leisure of planning your intervention so as to be an on-going dialogue. The long-term goal of your interventions is the same. Invite your child to step outside of their current situation and dispassionately examine all the issues, introduce critical information, and clear up misunderstandings. There are some additional goals that you may want to work into your interventions and casual conversations.

The first goal is to address objections in their proper order. Root causes should be addressed before all else. After the root cause or causes are addressed, try to meet each objection according to F.I.F.O. (first in, first out). What were the first objections that the wolves put forward that caused the proverbial first cracks in the dam? Experience has shown that these early arguments are often the most important. Subsequent objections were added during the indoctrination phases to shore up these original objections. Therefore, these subsequent arguments are usually of secondary importance.

Addressing the earliest most important arguments first will often make the secondary arguments fall apart.

A second goal may be to try to reconnect your child with their pre-recruitment personality. Remind them of the good times, about how things were *before* they were recruited. Try to keep these memories alive. Wolves will often tamper with their recruit's memories. They may learn about one or two sordid events in your child's past and over-exaggerate them. Eventually, if it is done frequently enough, the recruit begins to believe the exaggeration and suddenly their former-life was one of nothing but sin, misery, and woe. If a recruiter learns, for example, that your child once became drunk at a party, he may introduce your child to the group as someone who was once an alcoholic who changed after joining the group. The positive reinforcement from the exaggeration pushes the recruit to start buying into the lie. Sometimes recruits even embellish these memories so as to gain more approval from the wolf-pack. You may have already noticed a tendency in your child to recall only the worst things about his Catholic upbringing. The fact is that prior to recruitment, your child's life was not all darkness and woe any more than their new life with the wolves is a paradise.

The same type of memory tampering goes on with your child's present experience in the wolf pack. The more coercive groups will drill the idea into the mind of its members that they are the happiest, most enlightened, joyous people on the earth because of their membership in the pack. By proposing that all true members are always happy and joyous, the group pressures its members to convince themselves that they are happy and joyous. In cases such as this, parents should try to have a non-judgmental, heart-to-heart talk with their child about how they are really feeling. Allow your child to confide in you without using it as a weapon against them. Hopefully, your child will open up to you and share his true feelings about how things are going in their life. Your child may realize when they open up to you that things have not turned out as they expected, and he may ask for help.

As a final suggestion, try to use your child's jargon in your talks. Jargon can be a very powerful communication skill. Think of jargon as a secret password that by-passes defense mechanisms and loaded terminology. By your speaking like a wolf, your child may instinctively lower his or her defenses and passively accept what you have to say. Try to avoid using loaded terminology, because it has the opposite effect; it identifies you as the enemy, and your child will tune out anything you have to say no matter how true, persuasive, or logical it might be.

Apologetic Postures

How you engage your child in dialogue can be just as important at *what* you will talk about. Individuals have their own personality, obstacles, and belief-systems. Therefore, one approach doesn't fit all people when it comes to discussing the Faith. What I encourage apologists to do is to be familiar with the three main postures of a dialogue and choose the posture that best suits their situation. Using the correct dialogue posture can make it possible for you to gain a fair hearing from your child.

What are apologetic postures? An apologetic posture is the format within which your dialogue will take place. There are four basic postures, but only three are applicable here.

Head-to-Head

The first and most common posture is the head-to-head approach. The head-to-head posture is similar to a debate question-and-answer format where one debater raises an objection and his opponent answers it and then proposes another objection back at him! The head-to-head approach resembles a tennis match where each competitor tries to whiz past his opponent an unanswerable objection. Like tennis, the head-to-head posture promotes competition, and the goal of a dialogue that uses this posture is to score more points than your opponent and win.

The head-to-head posture has several benefits and drawbacks. On the plus side, speed is an obvious advantage in the head-to-head approach in that the dialogue moves very quickly. Speed also allows for more topics to be addressed in a relatively short time; a lot of territory can be covered quickly. The head-to-head posture also allows for a lot of agility in that it is very easy for the participants to steer the conversation in the direction that they wish to go. For example, whenever the point of discussion is in your court, so to speak, you have the ability to steer the conversation to other areas where your opponent may be able to respond. Both the speed and agility makes the format of the head-to-head posture very entertaining. Most public debates are essentially head-to-head contests. The speed and agility also make it an effective teaching tool in that through cross-examination a wide variety of topics can be covered very quickly. However, the strength of the head-to-head posture is also its weakness.

The most significant disadvantage to the head-to-head approach is that it produces a very shallow dialogue. While the verbal ping-pong match is going on, each of the participant's attention is directed towards what they are going to spring on their opponent next. They are not focused on considering the merits of what the opponent has argued. Serious objections, therefore, are not given due consideration. Shallow dialogues rarely produce a meeting of minds. Therefore, the head-to-head posture may not be the best posture for interventions, since you want your child to work through the information.

Although entertaining, the combative nature of the head-to-head approach is a very big disadvantage. The approach fosters an "us versus them" mentality, which is usually the last thing a parent would want his child to assume during an intervention. The atmosphere generated by this posture makes the frank recognition that your opponent had made a good point virtually impossible. Another disadvantage is the posture's topical agility. The head-to-head approach can make the topic of a conversation easy to steer, but it also gives the person you are dialoguing with the ability to steer the conversation wherever they'd like to go, too. Therefore, head-to-head dialogues tend *not* to stay on topic, but wildly swing from one topic to another. If you wish to make an argument that is based on more than two premises, good luck. Chances are you won't be able to draw a conclusion before the conversation moves on to something completely different.

Another factor that you may wish to consider when you are determining which posture will work best for your intervention is time. The head-to-head approach is not conducive to future discussions; both parties have essentially made their points, albeit briefly, and if your child is on the losing end of the conversation, he or she will not want to go back at it again. Therefore, the head-to-head approach is very well suited for one-time interventions, but is not a good approach if you wish to have an on-going dialogue. The next two postures may be a better choice.

Side-by-Side Posture

The side-by-side posture is very different from the first posture. Instead of firing objections at your opponent, you receive his objection and invite the objector to come along side you and examine the objection together. The following dialogue will illustrate how this posture works.

Annie: "The Catholic teaching on X flatly contradicts the Bible and here is why...."

Parent: "Before you continue, why don't you jot down on a piece of paper all the references that you are about to give me and I'll jot down a few for you. Then maybe we can examine each list on our own and meet again to share what we found?"

Annie: "Why do you want to do that?"

Parent: "Annie, I hold you and the Scriptures in such high regard that I want to prayerfully consider what you have to say, and I hope that you feel the same way about me. By comparing notes, maybe you can show me where I'm going wrong or maybe I might find something that you haven't considered either. After all, both of us want to follow what is true. Am I right?"

Annie: "I suppose so. I doubt that you'll be able to show me anything new. I've studied the Bible very thoroughly. But if it helps you, let's do it."

By committing to meet again, you've prolonged your discussion and also provided yourself with time to critique your child's objections and plan your next move. Together both of you, at the next meeting, will examine the material, not as opponents but as two people trying to get to the truth of the matter. Fight the temptation to back your child into a corner at this meeting; simply make the point and move on. Winning arguments isn't the goal. The real goal is to thoroughly work through the evidence and to allow your child to reevaluate their position.

When evidence is discovered that calls into question the honesty of the wolves, ask your child a question or two about how they could make such a mistake. Wolves try to impress upon their recruits that the group is extremely knowledgeable and its arguments are invincible. When it is discovered that the wolves have completely distorted a point of fact, your child should feel, at some level, that something is not quite right. How can the group be so knowledgeable and at the same time distort facts? Either the group's research is sloppy, which calls into question its reliability, or perhaps it knowingly distorted the facts, which calls into question its honesty. Ask questions that will bring these implications to the foreground. For example, one may say, "I'm surprised your friends didn't know this. They seemed to have understood other things fairly well. Why do you think they didn't tell you what the Church really taught?" Pause and give him time to think about what you asked. Regardless of how your child answers, don't beat him over the head with the point. Ask it and move on.

The side-by-side posture has a number of advantages. The most impressive advantage in using this posture is that discussions rarely become heated because the participant's attention is focused on understanding the material, not winning a debate. The second advantage to focusing on the material is that the topics that are addressed can be investigated in depth. When done correctly, the side-by-side posture can produce very informative and substantive discussions, which makes this posture very well-suited when the parent is considering doing many small interventions over a period of time.

Unlike the head-to-head posture, this posture is devoid of any pressure to use pre-fabricated answers or to bluster your way through an argument. There is no shame in saying, "I don't know. I'll have to look that up." In fact, admitting that you don't know something in this posture produces more material to go over in the next meeting. Being humble enough to admit that you don't have an answer will show that you respect your child's position and that you really want to hear and consider what they have to say. Usually gestures like this are reciprocated. Your child just might admit that he or she doesn't know something and that he will further consider what you have said further. The side-by-side posture, more than any other, makes it easy to share resources (*i.e.*, books, tapes, CDs, DVDs, radio shows, television shows). These items can be easily incorporated into your discussions. A parent can always say, "Boy, a professor on this CD really explains this point much better than I. Would you mind if we listened to it together and then you can let me know what you think?"

As good as the side-by-side posture is, it still suffers from a few disadvantages. The success of the side-by-side posture depends largely upon the zeal and sincerity of your child. The side-by-side posture essentially calls your child's bluff. It is like saying, "If you have the truth, then I want it too, *but first you must demonstrate it to me*." Some will take you up on the challenge while others will not. If your child has written you off as a hopeless cause, this posture will not work for you. Also, if your child has developed a superiority complex through his or her involvement with the wolves, the side-by-side approach will not appear attractive to your child at all. The side-by-side approach works best with kids who want to win their parents over to the group. They are willing to jump through any hoop to evangelize their parents, even if it means re-evaluating their own position.

Finally, the side-by-side posture has the disadvantage of being slow and time consuming; it requires both parties to have enough leisure time to research topics and get together for meetings. Free time is a scarce commodity for most people. However, measures can be taken to alleviate the time crunch. For example, discussions don't have to be in person. Conversation can take place over the phone or email, or even regular mail. Face-to-face meetings are always best, but any type of meeting is always better than no meeting.

Back-Peddling Posture

Certain wolf-packs instill in their recruits a worldview that they alone are in the light and everything else is in darkness; they alone have the truth and everyone else lives in error, and they are the teachers and non-group members have nothing instructive to tell them. One will usually encounter this type of mentality in pseudo-Christian groups like Jehovah's Witnesses, Mormons, and Christadelphians as well as some Christian groups such as some strict Calvinists, Church of Christ, and others.

If your child has this worldview, chances are the first two postures or apologetic approaches will be of little use. The head-to-head approach, if done well, may be helpful to break through the light versus darkness facade. The combative nature of the head-to-head posture usually makes these epiphanies rather rare. Moreover, it invites the use of canned answers and objection without much further consideration. The side-by-side is probably the least attractive to use when talking to a member whose worldview is so sharply divided. Your child may condescend to try this approach, but it will likely be done to try to humor you rather than to seriously look into the issues. Everyone is different so don't rule out the possibility of using the side-by-side with your child.

If your child can never honestly consider anything that you tell him about religion or consider any evidence that you bring to the table, the back-peddling posture might be the best way to gain a fair hearing.

What is the back-peddling posture? It is a combination of the head-to-head posture, in that it has an objection/response aspect to it and the side-by-side posture, in that it focuses the attention on the evidence. The back-peddling posture buys into the "all-enlightened" persona of your child by putting yourself in the position of the "uninformed" student. Unlike the head-to-head approach, you do not pose any objections; you only ask questions (as with the Socratic Method). Through a series of questions, you lead your child (backwards, if you will) to the conclusions that you want him to see. Let's use a dialogue to illustrate just how the back-peddling posture works. If your child has joined a group that denies that Jesus is God, you can ask him questions that will lead him to see that the group's reasoning doesn't explain or account for all of the evidence.

Child: "Jesus isn't God. Scripture nowhere makes such an assertion."

Parent: "Hmm. That's very interesting. I don't understand, though. Didn't St. Thomas call Jesus 'my Lord and my God' in John 20:28? If Jesus wasn't God, why did Thomas call him 'my Lord and *my God*'?"

Child: "Oh, that's a very common mistake. You see Thomas wasn't calling Jesus 'God.' Thomas was making an exclamation. He was saying, 'Oh, my lord and my God, it is really you, Jesus!' That's all he was saying."

[Having studied the question beforehand, the parent responds.]

Parent: "I see. But something doesn't seem to make sense to me. If what you say is true, wouldn't Thomas have used the Lord's name in vain?"

Child: "Well, I guess so, but you have to realize that Thomas wasn't perfect. Only Jesus was a perfect man."

Parent: "Ok. I see what you're trying to say, but that only confuses me more. Maybe you can clarify it for me. If Thomas did what you said, he would have broken one of God's commandments right there in front of Jesus. Why didn't Jesus rebuke Thomas? After all, if Jesus was a 'perfect man,' it would have been Jesus' duty to rebuke Thomas. Wouldn't it? But he doesn't. In fact, Jesus continues right along with his dialogue as if nothing offensive had happened. Why do you think he did that?"

Child: "Hmm. I'm not sure."

Notice how the parent used the back-peddling posture to lead the child to a point without posing any direct objections. The parent simply was asking questions for clarification and forcing his child to think through more deeply the explanation that he was giving. Eventually, the parent's questions began to move outside the standard responses that the child was taught to give and made the child realize that the wolves' explanation didn't accurately explain the passage.

The back-peddling posture can be very effective, but it requires preparation and research. You'll need to know beforehand what the canned responses to common objections will be and what the likely follow up answer will be to your response. Finding this information is not difficult. Groups that hold the "light versus darkness" worldview tend to use canned answers and responses. A good apologetic book, talk, or lecture series *dedicated to your child's group* will be a very valuable guide.

Knowledge is the key to success when using this posture. By knowing what counter-arguments will be launched, you can control where the discussion will go simply by asking the right questions. Most wolves will have a standard response and a standard rejoinder and that's it. Once you've gone outside of the standard rejoinder, your child will be in uncharted territory. Uncharted territory is the most valuable cognitive real-estate for your discussion to dwell. When your child runs out of canned answers, he or she is forced to think critically about what is being said. Critical thinking is good. The lack of critical thinking led your child to be with the wolves and an increase in critical thinking may get him out. Take your time and let him work through the problem.

Typically what happens with the back-peddling approach is that you'll be able to lead your child backwards into three or four very good questions. After the meeting, your child will consult with a recruiter on how best to answer your questions. The recruiters will most likely give a canned response. At this point, your questioning may pay dividends. By asking questions and dwelling in uncharted territory, your child may have begun to think critically about the group's beliefs. If the canned responses aren't very convincing to your child, your child might ask them further questions (after all, he or she is going to have to come back to you and defend the response he or she will give you). Wolves do not like persistent questions and they may suggest to your child to either cut off contact with you because you are ruining their faith, or that he or she may be happier elsewhere. Regardless of the immediate outcome, you've planted some very valuable seeds.

The advantages of the back-peddling posture are threefold: (1) it can help the person who believes they have the answers to everything to realize that they really don't know as much as they think, (2) shows the person that what they do know is really quite shallow and does not adequately explain or interpret all of the evidence; and (3) the posture helps jumpstart your child's critical thinking skills. Once your child begins to critically think through what he or she was taught, good things will begin to happen.

Apologetic postures can be very helpful in gaining a fair hearing from your child, even when your child is convinced that you have nothing useful to say. Choose the posture that best fits your situation. You can also switch from posture to posture whenever the situation calls for it. Whatever apologetic posture you do decide to take, the goal is to help your child reconsider his decision in light of all the evidence.

For more information on what to do to help your child who has already left the Faith, I recommend an excellent book by Patrick Madrid titled *Search and Rescue: How to Bring Your Family and Friends Into, or Back Into, the Catholic Church* (Sophia Institute Press: 2001). *Search and Rescue* will provide a good overview and go into further detail on all of the different aspects and dimension of rescuing your child or loved ones from anti-Catholic predators.

Appendix A –Essential Equipment for Wolf-proofing

Wolf-proofing parents need tools and resources to educate themselves and their children. These resources and tools can be broken down into three categories, namely a Catholic resource center, a Catholic entertainment center, and life lines. Let's explore what each of these tools are and what they should include.

Catholic Resource Center

In Chapter 3, a suggestion was made to designate a bookshelf or bookcase to function as the family's Catholic resource center. The resource center was to function as a one-stop location in the household where parents and children can consult various resources. It was also suggested that this bookcase be keep in a location that is well known to all in the family that way if your children ever have a question about the Faith, they know where to look up an answer.

What should your Catholic resource center include? The center should contain books and other resource materials that cover four basic areas of study :

Catechetical materials

Apologetic material (covering Theistic, Natural, Catholic, pseudo-Christian Apologetics and Bible Basics material mentioned in chapter 3)

Resources geared towards evangelism (books, DVDs, music, CDs.)

Resources for building critical thinking skills (introductions to logic, logical fallacies, and how to spot propaganda)

Appendix B will break down each of these categories into concrete recommendations that may help you with your teaching and skill-building exercises.

Once these main categories are covered, you may consider adding other books to further enhance your library. One suggestion is that you could have at least one or two good books on Church history or patristics.

Patristics: The study of the life and writings of the early Church Fathers.

Learning Church history gives the historical backdrop for what your children will learn in catechesis and it also enables them to familiarize themselves with the writings of the first centuries of the Church. The writings of the early Church fathers are a very important component in Catholic apologetics. Learning Church history also prevents wolves from distorting controversial events in history such as the Inquisition, the Crusades, and the Galileo affair.

Keep an eye on the headlines as well. Periodically, the news will dig up some old anti-Catholic lark and dress it up to make it seem like it is a new groundbreaking discovery. Like the swallows that return to Capistrano every year, certain magazines will run stories every Christmas and Easter that supposedly debunk Christianity. Invariably, these stories are nothing more than old arguments that have been refuted over and over again over the years. The same is true about the charge concerning the Catholic Church's actions during World War II, despite the fact that dozens of very good books, written by both Catholics and non-Catholics, have debunked these charges over and over again. The attacks continue to resurface every now and again. If you notice this phenomenon occurring, pick up a book or two that debunks the subject just to have on hand. If your children won't need it, your friends or neighbors who believe these charges might find it helpful. Appendix B will recommend a couple of books on the World War II topic.

Catholic Bible resources should also be added to your library. At the very minimum, your library should have at least one Catholic translation of the Bible, one Catholic Bible dictionary, and at least one book that serves as an introduction to Scripture. Again, Appendix B will provide some excellent recommendations for this area.

Finally, parents should also consider owning a copy of the Catholic Encyclopedia. A set such as the Catholic Encyclopedia can be pricey. If you keep your eyes open, you may spot a bargain either online or at used book sales.

The Catholic Encyclopedia is available free on the internet (**www.newadvent.org**). The online version is very serviceable. You can call me old-fashioned, but I still recommend having your children leafing through the printed set rather than surfing through it online. Besides the benefit of giving your children another reason not to be in front of their computer, physically searching an encyclopedia helps build good research skills. These skills will come in handy when they grow up and have to write research papers. Moreover, you can stumble upon new things that you'd otherwise never have known. Let's say that you are looking up the Papacy in an encyclopedia. While flipping the pages to find the article on the subject, your eye catches an interesting picture or unusual word. You take a few second to browse through the article and before you know it you've learned something new. Online browsing, for me at least, doesn't loan itself to that kind of accidental discovery. Most important of all, your children will learn the exact physical location of where they can find the answers to thousands of questions. Unless they use a particular website often, they may forget about this wonderful resource. If you can afford to buy a Catholic Encyclopedia, pick up a set. If your budget is too tight, use the online Catholic encyclopedia and dedicate the money you've saved towards purchasing other resources.

Building a Good Catholic Entertainment Library

Welcome to the Information Age. Where or how information is presented can influence how much credence people give to what is being said. For better or worse, television and radio have become the pinnacles of authoritative information. If a friend or loved one told you that the value of a dollar has dropped to an all time low, you may or may not believe them; but if that same person appeared on television and said the same thing, you'd probably believe him. The major media has become our standard for valuable information. If an idea isn't broadcast on television or radio, it's probably not that important. Children are particularly susceptible to this idea.

Therefore, it is important for parents to make sure that there is good Catholic programming (or Catholic-friendly programming) on their television and radios. Not only does Catholic programming show your children that Catholicism is important because it is broadcast, but a healthy diet of good programs can enrich and entertain you and your family.

Several years ago, the only movies available from a Catholic perspective were the old classics like "A Man for All Seasons" and "The Song of Bernadette." Catholic media has grown exponentially since our childhood and so has its quality. There are Catholic children's programs, cartoons, dramas, historical dramas, fiction, and documentaries as well. Parents should take advantage of the wide variety of choices made available to them.

Bottom line

A parent reading this section may think, "Yes, I need to have good programming on hand, but I'm not going to run out to the store and buy hundreds of movies. What are the essentials that I should have?" Start with a couple of the classics, like I just mentioned, "A Man for All Seasons" and "The Song of Bernadette." Do a little browsing and when something interests you, pick it up. I would suggest that when you are browsing for a DVD online that you surf the website of a good, solid Catholic publisher or retailer. That way you know that the movies listed are theologically solid. Appendix B will supply the names and contact information for Catholic publishers and distributors. After the classics are covered, pick out a few age appropriate DVDs for your children. If you have young children there are cartoons and youth adult shows.

Your entertainment library doesn't have to be totally Catholic. You certainly can include other programs that are conducive to building a good Catholic worldview. There are hundreds of purely secular movies that have great storylines which operate within a Judeo-Christian moral universe. When your child grows older and you've begun to train them to think critically, other media can be allowed under close supervision. Remember, part of wolf-proofing is to teach children not to receive information passively. Preview your movies and ask questions about them afterwards.

Be careful that you practice what you preach. Be careful not to insist that your children watch only good solid programming and then after you've sent them to bed you put on trash television for yourself. Use discernment in the programs you watch when the kids aren't around. Do they have some redeeming quality in them that contributes to your well being and spiritual growth? If it doesn't, why are you watching it? Enough said.

How can a family on a limited budget put together all these resources?

Don't take a chance on purchasing books with which you are unfamiliar. I've wasted hundreds of dollars and thousands of hours sifting through poor quality books and other materials. Appendix B will help you avoid making the same mistakes that I did. If there was a fire and I lost all of my books and resources, I would begin rebuilding my library using the books on my recommendation list. There is no fluff on the list; all the material is solid and very useable.

Several of the books on the recommendation list are out of print and getting out of print books can be expensive. If you wish to pick up these books, there are several online services that you can consult to get a price quote. These online used book services pool the inventories from hundreds of used bookstores worldwide and their on-line search options usually allow the results of your search to be sorted according to the asking price. Sometimes you can get a very good used book for only a few dollars, but be careful to take into consideration the shipping costs. A book may cost only a few dollars, but if it has to be shipped from overseas the postage may take the book out of your price range.

Another way you can pick up used books for a very low price is through used book sales at your local public library. I've found these sales to be a goldmine of great resources at incredibly low prices. You can pick up piles of books, bibles, dictionaries, and devotionals at these sales for a dollar or fifty cents each.

Library sales also sometimes sell DVDs and videotapes. There is also Catholic broadcasting media that you can tap into. If you have cable television or a satellite dish, there is the Eternal Word Television Network, which broadcasts good, solid Catholic programming twenty-four hours a day, seven days a week. E.W.T.N. also has a radio network and broadcasts on short wave. Another growing network is Ave Maria Radio, which produces several very fine programs that are worth tuning in to. There are several smaller local Catholic programs on the radio as well. Check the internet to see if there is a Catholic radio station in your listening area and tune them in.

Lifelines

A story was once told me about a reporter who asked Albert Einstein for his phone number. Einstein picked up a telephone book, looked up the phone number, and gave it to the reporter. "Don't you know your own phone number?" asked the stunned reporter. Einstein answered that a smart man doesn't need to know everything; he only needs to know where to find the answers. This story, whether true or fictitious, has always given me comfort in my work as an apologist: You cannot always know the answer to every question, but you can know *where* to find the answer. The best way to find the answer to a difficult question is to use a lifeline. What's a lifeline?

A lifeline is a person with special expertise in a given field, or it could be your Catholic Resource Center, or a particular library, or a trusted website. In fact, the book that you are reading right now can function as a lifeline. Whenever you are stumped on a question or you don't understand something that is being discussed, a lifeline can either give you the answer or help direct you to where you can find the answer.

Human lifelines are usually the most helpful, but I would suggest that you use this type of lifeline as an avenue of last resort. Most people who have a certain expertise in an area of study are usually pretty busy people and you don't want to waste their time unless you have no other recourse.

The pecking order for using lifelines should be something like this. First, consult your Apologetic Resource Center for the answer. If you don't have the material on hand, look online for an answer. There are several good Catholic websites and ministries that have tons of information to browse. Appendix B will give you the contact information and website addresses of some very good Catholic websites to consult. You can also go to my website (**www.HandsOnApologetics.com**) and look at the online apologetic library section, which contains hyperlinks to a wide variety of online resources. If you have no luck online, you may want to make a trip to your local public library or seminary library---someone there may help you find your answer. If all of the above fails, it's time to make the call to your lifeline.

How do I find a person to be my lifeline? A friend who is very adept in Catholic theology may be helpful or someone who is a well-seasoned apologist. Priests, deacons, seminary teachers and religious also have a wealth of information, but they time usually at a premium so they may be able to help you by suggesting other people that you can contact for help.

Perhaps one of the best and easiest lifelines to access is an apostolate headquartered in San Diego, California, called Catholic Answers. In addition to a daily live radio show that takes questions live from callers, Catholic Answers also has a help line for people off the air as well. Their website also includes an abundance of material, tracts, and very large forums that discuss almost every subject under the sun.

If you need help locating someone who is knowledgeable regarding a particular group, another Catholic apostolate named The Coming Home Network International might help. The Coming Home Network is an outreach for non-Catholic clergy and lay ministers who are interested in becoming Catholic. They may be able to help you find someone to consult on a particular denomination, church, sect, or cult. Another helpful and popular resource that you may wish to subscribe to is Patrick Madrid's "Envoy" Magazine. "Envoy" is a flashly, fun, and solid resource for the whole family on apologetics, evangelism, and Catholic life in general. Contact information for the Coming Home Network, Catholic Answers, and "Envoy" magazine can be found in Appendix C of this book.

Lifelines are probably the most important tools a Catholic parent can have. They give you a sense of confidence and security when you are learning or discussing subjects that you may not know well. Remember, if you don't know the answer, you should know where to find the answer. Good lifelines can direct you.

Appendix B – Resources and Recommendations

Recommendations for your apologetic library. Out of print items will be marked with a single asterisks(*) and non-Catholic resources will be marked with two asterisks(**).

Catechesis – Parent's Resources

Catechism of the Catholic Church: Second Edition (Doubleday Religion, 2003)

Vatican Council II, Vol. 1: The Conciliar and Postconciliar Documents, Austin Flannery (Costello Pub Co , 1975)

Fundamentals of Catholic Dogma, Ludwig Ott (TAN Books and Publishers, 2009)

Catechesis – Children's Resources

A Pocket Catechism for Kids, Kris D. Stubna and Mike Aquilina (Our Sunday Visitor, 2001).

Father McBride's Teen Catechism Teacher Guide: Based on the Catechism of the Catholic Church, Alfred McBride (Our Sunday Visitor, 1996).

Theistic Apologetics – Parent's Resources

Handbook of Christian Apologetics: Hundreds of Answers to Crucial Questions, Peter Kreeft and Fr. Ronald Tacelli (InterVarsity Press, 1994).

Additional reading:

* *On the Third Day*, Sir Arnold Lunn (The Newman Book Shop Westminster, MD, 1945).

***The Case for a Creator: A Journalist Investigates Scientific Evidence that Points Toward God*, Lee Strobel (Zondervan, 2005).

Theistic Apologetics – Children's Resources

Pocket Handbook of Christian Apologetics, Peter Kreeft and Fr. Ronald Tacelli (InterVarsity Press, 2003).

Fundamentals of the Faith: Essays in Christian Apologetics, Peter Kreeft (Ignatius Press, 1988) – Recommend for the sections on the existence of God and the uniqueness of Christ.

Catholic Apologetics: God, Christianity, and the Church (A Course in Religion), Fr. John Laux, (TAN Books and Publishers, 2009).

***The Miracle of Lourdes, the Complete True Story About the World Famous Shrine*, Ruth Cranston (Popular Library, 1957) – Cranston is a Protestant, but the book is very fair and respectful to the Catholic Faith.

Additional Reading

**Lourdes: A History of its Apparitions and Miracles*, Georges Bertrin, Trans. Mrs. Philip Gibbs (Kegan, Paul, Trench, Tubner, 1908) – available free online. Contains detailed analyses of a few miracles.

Natural or Christian Apologetics – Parent's Resources

**Beyond a Reasonable Doubt*, Fr. G. H. Duggan, S.M., (St. Paul Books and Media, 1987).

**The Case for Christ: A Journalist's Personal Investigation of the Evidence for Jesus*, Lee Strobel, (Zondervan, 1998).

Natural or Christian Apologetics – Children's Resources

Catholic Apologetics: God, Christianity, and the Church (A Course in Religion), Fr. John Laux, (TAN Books and Publishers, 2009). – Recommended Above.

Catholic Apologetics – Parent's Resources

Catholicism and Fundamentalism: The Attack on "Romanism" by "Bible Christians", Karl Keating, (Ignatius Press, 1988).

The Gospel According to James McCarthy: A Catholic Response to James McCarthy's The Gospel According to Rome, Gary Michuta (Grotto Press, 2003).

Additional Reading:

Radio Replies, Frs. Leslie Rumble and Charles Carty (3 volumes-sold separately) (Tan Book and Publishers, 1979) – Hundreds of concise questions and answers. Some out of date, most replies still very applicable).

Nuts & Bolts: A Practical Guide for Explaining and Defending the Catholic Faith, Timothy Staples (Basilica Press, 1999).

Theology and Sanity, Frank Sheed (Ignatius Press, 1993).

Bible Proofs for Catholic Truths: A Source Book for Apologists and Inquirers, David Armstrong (Sophia Institute Press, 2009).

The One-Minute Apologist, David Armstrong (Sophia Institute Press, 2007).

150 Bible Verses Every Catholic Should Know, Patrick Madrid (Servant Books, 2007).

Catholic Apologetics – Children's Resources

Beginning Apologetics: How to Explain and Defend the Catholic Faith (Booklet), Frank Chacon and Jim Burnham

Catholic Apologetics: God, Christianity, and the Church (A Course in Religion), Fr. John Laux, (TAN Books and Publishers, 2009) – Recommended Above.

Theology for Beginners, Frank Sheed (Servant Books, 1982).

Evangelism – Parent's Resources

Life of Christ, Fulton J. Sheen (Image Books, 1977).

This is My Body. This is My Blood; Miracles of the Eucharist, Bob and Penny Lord, Volumes 1 and 2 (Journeys of Faith, 1982).

Additional Reading

Surprised by Truth: 11 Converts Give the Biblical and Historical Reasons for Becoming Catholic, Patrick Madrid (Basilica Press, 1994).

Moments of Grace: Inspiring Stories from Well-known Catholics, Al Kresta and Nick Thomm (Servant Books, 2008).

All Things Guy: A Guide to Becoming a Man that Matters, Teresa Tomeo (Bezalel Books, 2009).

All Things Girl: Modern and Modest, Teresa Tomeo (Bazalel Books, 2009).

Evangelism – Children's Resources

New Picture Book of Saints: Illustrated Lives of the Saints for Young and Old, Saint Joseph Edition (Hardcover), Lawrence Lovasik – For younger children

Butler's Lives of the Saints: New Saints And Blesseds (Butler's Lives of the Saints (Numbered)) (Hardcover), Alban Butler (Liturgical Press; 2005).

Good Catholic Movies For Evangelism (Classics)

A Man for All Seasons (1966) Starring: Paul Scofield, Wendy Hiller, Robert Shaw, and Leo McKern DVD 2007.

Don Bosco, Starring: Ben Gazzarra (Salesiana Publishers) (VHS, DVD)

The Song of Bernadette (1943), Starring: Jennifer Jones, Charles Bickford, William Eythe, and Vincent Price (VHS, DVD).

The Passion of Joan of Arc, Starring: Maria Falconetti, Eugene Silvain, André Berley, and Maurice Schutz (Silent Movie, DVD).

The Miracle of Our Lady of Fatima, Starring: Gilbert Roland, Angela Clarke, Susan Whitney, and Sherry Jackson (DVD).

Quo Vadis? (1951) Directed by Mervyn LeRoy Starring: Robert Taylor, Deborah Kerr, Peter Ustinov.

Good Catholic / Christian Movies for Evangelism (Modern)

The Passion of the Christ Starring: James Caviezel, Monica Bellucci Director: Mel Gibson (2004)– Adult viewing

No Price too High & Dinner with Alex Jones: Pentecostal minister and now Catholic deacon tells why he became Catholic (Ninaveh Crossing)

NARNIA: The Lion The Witch and the Wardrobe (2005)

Champions of Faith: Baseball Edition; John Morales (Catholic Exchange)

Bella (2006) (Warning: Adult Content).

The 13th Day (Ignatius Press, 2009) – On the miracle of Fatima

Building Critical Thinking – Parent's Resources

Noise: How Our Media-saturated Culture Dominates Lives and Dismantles Families (Paperback), Teresa Tomeo (Ascension Press, 2007).

How the Catholic Church Built Western Civilization (Hardcover), Thomas E. Wood (Regnery Publishing Inc., 2005).

** **Introduction to Critical Thinking*, W.H. Werkmeister (Lincoln, Nebraska: Johnsen Publishing Company), 1948. – Great section on logical fallacies and an even better section on identifying propaganda.

Resources for Bible Basics – Parent's Resources

Where We Got the Bible: Our Debt to the Catholic Church, Henry Graham (TAN Books and Publishers, 2004).

Why Catholic Bibles Are Bigger: The Untold Story of the Lost Books of the Protestant Bible, Gary Michuta (Grotto Press, 2006).

Four Witnesses: The Early Church In Her Own Words, Rod Bennett (Ignatius Press, 2002).

Catholic Apologetics Today, Fr. William Most (TAN Books and Publishers, 1986).

Faith of the Early Fathers, 3 volumes, edited William A. Jurgens (Liturgical Press, 1980).

Making Sense Out of Scripture: Reading the Bible As the First Christians Did, Mark Shea (Basilica Press, 1999).

Resources for Bible Basics – Children's Resources

Understanding The Scriptures: A Complete Course On Bible Study (The Didache Series) (Hardcover), Dr. Scott Hahn (Midwest Theological Forum, 2005).

Studies on Specialized Subjects

General Protestant

Roots of the Reformation, Karl Adams (Coming Home Resources, 2000).

Church of Christ

Christ in His Fullness, Bruce Sullivan (Coming Home Network, 2007).

Jehovah's Witnesses

Answering Jehovah's Witnesses, Jason Evert (Catholic Answers, 2006).

**(*Index of Watchtower Errors 1879 to 1989*, David Reed (Baker Books, 1990). (Protestant)

** Jehovah's Witness Literature: A Critical Guide to Watchtower Publications, David Reed, (Baker Pub Group, 1993). (Protestant)

** *How to Rescue Your Loved One from the Watchtower*, David A. Reed (Baker Pub Groups, 1989). (Protestant)

Mormons (Church of Jesus Christ of Latter-day Saints).

Inside Mormonism: What Mormons Really Believe, Isaiah Bennett (Catholic Answers, 1999).

When Mormons Call, Isaiah Bennett (Catholic Answers, 1999).

***The Changing World of Mormonism*, Jerald and Sandra Tanner (Moody Press,) – (available free online at Utah Lighthouse Ministry). (Protestant)

New Age Movement

Oprah: Televangelist Of The New Age Deception (Catholic Answers) CD set.

Catholics and the New Age: How Good People Are Being Drawn into Jungian Psychology, the Enneagram, and the Age of Aquarius, Fr. Mitch Pacwa (Servant Publications, 1992).

Atheism

Answering the New Atheism: Dismantling Dawkins' Case Against God, Scott Hahn and Benjamin Wiker (Emmaus Road Publishing, 2008).

10 Books That Screwed Up the World: And 5 Others That Didn't Help, Benjamin Wiker (Regnery Press, 2008).

Secularism / Anti-Catholicism

***The New Anti-Catholicism: The Last Acceptable Prejudice*, by Philip Jenkins (Oxford University Press, 2004) – written by an Episcopalian.

Islam

Islam and Christianity - by Father Mitch Pacwa and Daniel Ali (5 CD set) available at Crossroads Initiative (http://www.crossroadsinitiative.com).

The Politically Incorrect Guide to Islam (and the Crusades), Robert Spencer (Regnery Publishing, Inc., 2005).

The Truth About Muhammad: Founder of the World's Most Intolerant Religion, Robert Spencer (Regnery Publishing, Inc.), 2007.

Appendix C – Ministries and other Resources

Catholic Answers / This Rock Magazine (Radio, Magazine, and Online Resources)

P. O. Box 199000, San Diego, California 92159
Contact: 619-387-7200
Website (forum): www.Catholic.com

Patrick Madrid / Envoy Magazine (Author, Radio, Magazine, and Online Resources)

PO Box 640 Granville, Ohio 43023
Contact: 740-345-2705
Website (forum): patrickmadrid.com/
Email: Info@patrickmadrid.com

John Martignoni / The Bible Christian Society (Radio, Audio, and Online Resources)

PO Box 424
Pleasant Grove, Alabama 35127
Website : www.biblechristiansociety.com

Gary Michuta (Author, Online Resources)

Website: www.HandsOnApologetics.com
Email: gmichuta@hotmail.com

David Armstrong / Biblical Defense of Catholicism (Author, Online Resources)

Website: http://socrates58.blogspot.com/

Stephen Ray (Author, Video, Audio, and Online Resources)

Website (Forum): www.catholicconvert.com

The Coming Home Network International (Television, Radio, Online Resources)

P.O. Box 8290, Zanesville, OH 43702
Phone: (800) 664-5110, (740) 450-1175
Website: www.chnetwork.org
Information: info@chnetwork.org

Steve Clifford / Transporter Info Services (Online Mormon Resources)

Website: www.transporter.com/apologia/index.htm
Email: www.transporter.com/index.htm

Jeffery and Kathy Schwehm (The Fellowship of Catholic Ex-Jehovah's Witnesses)

4802 B S. Amanda Lane
Sheboygan, Wisconsin 53081
Contact: (920) 783-0376
Website: www.catholicxjw.coml
Email: jschwehm@catholicxjw.com

Eternal Word Television Network (Television, Radio, Online Resources)

5817 Old Leeds Rd, Birmingham, Alabama 35210
Contact: (205) 271- 2900
Website: www.ewtn.com

Saint Joseph Communication (Video and Audio Resources)

P.O. Box 720, West Covina, CA 91793
Toll Free: 800-526-2151
In California: 626-331-3549

Saint Joseph Communications

P.O. BOX 733, Lloydminster, SK, Canada, S9V 1V1
Toll Free: 877-871-2893
Website: www.saintjoe.com
Email: info@saintjoe.com

Daniel Ali (Video and Audio Resources on Islam)

Website: www.danielali.org/index.html

Robert Spencer (Author, Online Resources on Islam)

http://www.jihadwatch.org

Non-Catholic Ministries

The following resources are recommended with caution since some of their material does not comport with Catholicism and may be antagonistic to it. Outside of these defects, they do provide very helpful information and research.

Utah Lighthouse Ministry (On Mormonism) (Publisher and Online Resources)

P.O. BOX 1884, Salt Lake City, UT 84110
Website: www.utlm.org

The Utah Lighthouse Ministry is an excellent storehouse of information about doctrine and practices of Mormons. It does, on occasion, allow anti-Catholic authors who are not as diligent in their research to contribute information.

Randall Watters, Free Minds Inc. (Jehovah Witnesses, Counter-cult) (Author, Online Resources)

Website: www.freeminds.org

Randall's website is an excellent resource for out-to-date information on the Watchtower Bible and Tract Soceity. He also is on the cutting edge of new methods to rescue JWs from the grips of the Soceity. Although some people on his forums are anti-Catholic, I have found Randall to be fair and even-handed in regards to our Faith.

Steven Hassan / Freedom of Mind (Counter-Cult) (Author and Online Resouces)

http://www.freedomofmind.com/

Steven Hassan is recommended for parents whose children had been recruited into smaller or lesser known sects or cults.

Catholic Publishers

The Grotto Press

3771 Barberry Circle
Wixom, MI 48393
Phone (877) 247-6886
FAX (248) 926-5950
Website: www.GrottoPress.org

Grotto Press has graciously agreed to make a special section on their website to offer many of the recommended titles listed in this book.

Ignatius Press

P.O. Box 1339
Ft. Collins, CO 80522
1-800-651-1531
Website: www.ignatius.com

Our Sunday Visitor

200 Noll Plaza
Huntington, IN 46750.
Toll-free: 1-800-348-2440
Phone: 260-356-8400
www.osv.com
osvbooks@osv.com

Sophia Institute Press

Box 5284
Manchester, NH 03108
Telephone: 1-800-888-9344
1-603-641-9344
www.sophiainstitute.com
orders@sophiainstitute.com

TAN Books and Publishers

PO Box 410487
Charlotte, NC 28241
(800) 437-5876
http://www.tanbooks.com/

Servant Books

Servant Books
P.O. Box 7015
Ann Arbor, MI 48107
Fax: 734-332-0131
www.Servantbooks.org

Websites (Free Material)

There has been an exponential growth in the amount of older public domain books that are available free on the Internet in PDF and other formats. You can save a lot of time and money by consulting these websites. The author's website, www.HandsOnApologetics.com, also contains links to many of these resources in a section called "The Apologetic Desktop."

Google Books – Contains thousands of books on various subjects.

www.google.com/books

New Advent Website- Contains the Old Catholic Encyclopedia, St. Thomas Aquinas' Summa Theologica, the early fathers of the Church, the Douay-Rheims Bible, and dozens of Church documents.

www.newadvent.org

Catholic Answers – Contains hundreds of free tracts as well as excellent downloadable radio programs produced by Catholic Answers Live. Lots of helpful advice as well.

www.Catholic.com

Internet Archive – Contains thousands of downloadable books and public domain articles.

www.archive.com

WorldCAT – Search the world's libraries for books. You may find needed resources at your local library. If the book you would like is not available at a library close to you, many libraries participate in a loaning program. You may be able to request a title to be loaned to a library close to you so that you may read it. Check your local library for this service.

www.worldcat.org

Made in the USA
Middletown, DE
22 August 2017